THE NEW BUSINESS JOURNALISM

OTHER BOOKS BY DON GUSSOW

Divorce Corporate Style
The New Merger Game
Chaia Sonia

The New Business Journalism

An Insider's Look at the Workings
of America's Business Press

by DON GUSSOW
founder of Magazines For Industry, Inc.

Harcourt Brace Jovanovich, Publishers
San Diego, New York, London

Copyright © 1984 by Don Gussow

Library of Congress Cataloging in Publication Data

Gussow, Don.
   The new business journalism.

   Bibliography: p.
   Includes index.
   1. Journalism, Commercial.   I. Title.
PN4784.C7G87   1984   338.4'7070486   83-18473
ISBN: 0-15-165202-3

Printed in the United States of America

First Edition

A B C D E

2234006

For Charlie Mill, the former
president of the American
Business Press, Inc., and my
colleagues, the members of the ABP

Contents

PART II: STRUCTURE & FUNCTION OF THE BUSINESS PRESS

PART V: PUBLIC RELATIONS AND
ADVERTISING
IN BUSINESS COMMUNICATIONS

APPENDIXES

Preface

Several years ago I was one of four panelists at a career opportunity seminar for senior students in the journalism department of a large urban university. I represented the specialized business press, while the other three panelists represented a large city daily newspaper, a successful consumer magazine, and one of the three largest national broadcasting companies. Each panelist discussed the opportunities for journalism graduates in his or her field, touching on beginning positions and salaries, the possibilities for growth on the job, and the likelihood of reaching the top of the career ladder.

In a question and answer session following my speech, I was surprised to learn how little the members of this particular graduating class knew about the field of specialized business publications. It soon became apparent why these budding reporters and editors were ignoring the specialized business press as a career option. Knowing nothing or little about this branch of journalism and the opportunities it offered, it was easy for them to look to the more glamorous areas of communications for lifetime careers. After all, they read newspapers and consumer magazines, watched television, and listened to the radio. But when was the last time they had picked up a copy of the *Oil and Gas Journal, Machine Design*, or the *Engineering News Record*, three of the top 10 specialized business periodicals in the United States? The students seemed to be enchanted with highly visible television commentators, such as Walter Cronkite, Dan Rather, Mike Wallace, Barbara Walters, and David Brinkley, and with well-known columnists from the large urban dailies, such as James Reston, David Broder, and George Will. What these young men and women did not know was that there are great opportunities for growth and fulfillment as well as for public visibility for highly motivated journalists in the business press; and that in rejecting the business press, they were crossing off—according to a recent *Folio* survey—fully half of the publication job market in the United States.

This book is written not only for those just entering journalism who must decide on a direction to follow, but also for those currently working in the business press who wish to have a broader perspective of their jobs. In the pages that follow I have attempted to update information about the various forms of business communication.

While the book deals with business journalism in general, most of it is devoted to the work of the specialized business press and its effect on the business community and, indirectly, on consumers. Information featured in the more than 5,600 specialized business periodicals in the United States and Canada is, after all, of vital importance to the consumer, since the specialized business press is concerned with the production and marketing of everything from wearing apparel to electronics and computers, from candy and snacks to the technology of oceanography and the new science of gene splicing.

The book is divided into five parts dealing, respectively, with the history of business communications, the structure and function of the business press, growth areas, functions outside the communications role of the business press such as marketing and merchandising, and the role of public relations and advertising in business communications.

Appendixes include a glossary of terms, a suggested training program for circulation personnel, a list of colleges and universities offering courses in business journalism, a list of selected business publication publishers, and a bibliography.

Of special interest to those concerned with the administration of specialized business periodicals is Part II, Structure and Function of the Business Press. Not only are normal editorial practices and production procedures covered, but considerable space is devoted to the economics of the business press, budgeting, and the duties of the advertising and the circulation departments.

Among other issues treated are new developments in electronic communications, the importance of the business communicator as a corporate spokesperson, the role of the public relations practitioner, and the growth of business periodicals devoted to specific geographic areas. A separate chapter describes the steps required to launch a new specialized business periodical.

I hope that this book will stimulate greater interest in business journalism on the part of journalism students, the academic community, and the media in general, as well as the business and professional communities served by the specialized business press. Business journalism is an exciting field, and those in it have an important task—describing and interpreting the complex and dynamic world of commerce and industry. If this book can convey even a vague notion of the sense of fulfillment inherent in the job of the business journalist, it will have served its purpose.

PART I

Background

Early History of the Business Press and Current Significant Developments: An Overview

Although business journalism has reached an unprecedented degree of excellence and maturity in recent years, especially in those firms that incorporate new communications technology, it continues to change, and in many ways dramatically. Today's business press is radically different than it was ten years ago. Indeed, so striking have been the changes during the past decade that nothing resembling them was even imagined from the 1940s through the 1960s. And there is every reason to believe that this "new" business journalism is poised for even greater innovation and growth.

The dynamism that business journalism now exhibits has generated interest and excitement in the entire communications field. While the effects of the new business journalism are now being felt in all areas of creative communications, they have had particular impact in at least two areas: business-news reporting and the overall size of the business press. Expanded and improved forms of business-news coverage are evident in all media, but especially in the daily newspapers; and business periodicals—the trade papers of an earlier era—have proliferated in response to the ever-more-specialized needs of business and industry.

Substantial growth has encouraged business journalists to take advantage of modern communications technology in order to keep pace with their respective fields. Among other things, purveyors of business information now offer access to computerized information banks and instant delivery of business news through electronic media. Nor has the printed page remained static. The technology of typesetting and printing has become increasingly sophisticated. In the United States the lumbering Linotype machine has been replaced by high-speed, computerized photocomposition. In addition, use of word processors spreads daily. On the whole, improved technology and enhanced emphasis on graphics and design have made the printed page more attractive and readable.

While broadcast journalism has lagged behind other media in reporting business news, more time is being devoted to the business scene on both radio and television, and the scope of their coverage has broadened considerably. The major networks already have special business-news departments. Interviews with economists and business specialists are also increasingly featured. Though the public service channels lead the networks in airing business features, commercial networks and local and regional stations are beginning to offer special business programming as well. Still, it is the printed page, plus the "on-order" transmission of business news by electronic means, that will dominate the delivery of news and other information to the business and industrial communities in the years ahead.

Characterizing the "New" Business Press

What precisely is this "new" business journalism and how does it differ from the profession as practiced prior to the 1970s? For one thing, business journalism has at last become a profession— not only with respect to the widespread application of standards of quality, but also in the development of first-rate editorial material and in upgraded requirements for employees. Its new status is seen in the improved attitude toward the profession shown by academia, especially by schools and departments of journalism. It is reflected in the new-found sophistication of the layout, art, and advertising to be found in the business press.

Prior to the 1970s the scene was very different. In the early part of this century specialized business periodicals, then called trade papers, were, with few exceptions, basically a hodgepodge. While improvements were made in the 1950s and 1960s, it was not until the 1970s that large numbers of business magazines took major steps to revamp their image and operations. As a measure of the rather haphazard approaches that existed before the seventies, one may note that no particular requirements had been established in the industry for the hiring and training of new editors. Moreover, not one school or department of journalism offered specific programs in business journalism. Today an increasing number of institutions do offer such programs, or at least courses in business journalism. Many schools have established internships with publishing companies. Internships generally involve the part-time or temporary hiring of students who plan careers in business journalism. Often these students have the opportunity to rotate through a variety of publications and to work in almost all phases of magazine work, including reporting, writing, and various aspects of production.

In addition to improving its editorial personnel, the business press has upgraded editorial quality by introducing electronic and data-base publishing (discussed later in this book).

Careers in the Business Press

A significant difference exists between the consumer press and the specialized business press in terms of the number of opportunities open to people of exceptional talent and ambition. In the consumer press, where there is more extreme competition, only a few individuals ever reach the summit. In the business press, on the other hand, a much greater number are afforded the chance to reach various peaks—which can include becoming a key executive (and often substantial shareholder) of a specialized business press operation or even owner of a publishing company. Although the rewards (both in salary and in public exposure) are greater for the few who become successful in the consumer press, the chance for fulfillment and an interesting life-style are present in both areas, with perhaps a bit less pressure in the specialized business press.

The consumer press—including newspapers, magazines, and broadcasting—also demands, in general, a different approach to the job than that taken in the business press. Members of the consumer press must both inform and entertain the public—and at times entertaining is more important than informing. The business press, on the other hand—and particularly the specialized business periodical—has the basic objective of informing its readership of developments, innovations, and news current in a particular industry or group of related fields. A periodical that deals with the manufacture and marketing of steel, for example, must provide specialized information about this industry in all its aspects. A magazine that covers the packaging field deals with the packaging of virtually any product. Thus, unlike their colleagues in the consumer press, who are often expected to be generalists, business journalists are required to be specialists—to possess intimate knowledge of the workings of the industry (or group of industries) they cover.

The Beginnings of the Business Press

Business communications in Europe received its major advance with the advent of printing in the fifteenth century. In the United States, business communications, basically in the form of trade papers, originated in the eighteenth century, but it was not until the second half of the twentieth century that the field began to mature; from then on, the growth and importance of business communications accelerated.

Early Trade Papers

The *Price Current*, started in the mid-eighteenth century, represented the first true business publication or trade paper in colonial America. Essentially a listing of prices of imported and exported products, it provided current information for importers and exporters, as well as for manufacturers and dealers.

A number of such *Currents* were established in the country. Among the better known were the *South Carolina Price Current*, founded in 1774, a 6-by-17-inch, two-column, single sheet listing prices of a number of commodities. Another was the *Philadelphia Price Current*, launched in 1788, which had a similar single-page format.

The General Shipping and Commercial List, published in New York, was established in 1815. It was later converted to a more inclusive business daily and the name changed to the *Journal of Commerce*. It is still published today, the only one of the original "currents" to have survived.

While a few other trade papers began in the early 1800s, it was not until the middle of the nineteenth century that they started to flourish. "Trade paper" is perhaps a too-generous description of these early four-page tabloids, which were crudely assembled with hand-set type and showed no particular uniformity of design or writing. The term "flourishing" is also used with reservation. Although the early trade papers increased in number, many died in infancy, and only a few reached maturity. Nevertheless, this was a critical time for early business publications.

Most early trade papers were directed to retailers. Prior to the Industrial Revolution, few manufacturing businesses existed, and those that did were based on manual modes of production. Merchants dominated the business scene, and the early trade papers served their needs. One of the first such business periodicals to emerge was *The Merchants' Magazine and Commercial Review*, a monthly first published in July 1839.

As American industry began to grow, so did the numbers of new trade papers. The shipping business was among the first to grow, and several trade papers were soon launched (in the early 1800s) to serve this field. The railroad industry followed (the first steam locomotive was introduced in 1830). Shortly thereafter, several railroad periodicals appeared, including the *American Railroad Journal* and the *Railroad Advocate*. These two periodicals actually preceded a fully operating railroad.

It should be noted that historically the appearance of trade papers has tended to accompany the beginnings of industries. Some trade papers actually created or aided the development of emerging industries, trades, and businesses.

It was not until the mid-1850s, however, that an onrush of trade papers occurred. Following are a few examples:

- *Railway Age* (still published by Simmons-Boardman Publishing Corporation) was launched in 1856. This was one of a dozen railroad trade journals to make an appearance from the 1830s to the 1860s.
- *United States Tobacco Journal* (started as a weekly, now published biweekly with much coverage of ancillary products) was introduced in 1874 by Oscar Hammerstein, a famous theatrical figure (and grandfather of the twentieth-century lyricist), who liked to smoke cigars.
- *American Machinist* was established in 1877 by Miller & Bailey. It is still published by McGraw-Hill, Inc.
- The *Confectioners Journal*, a four-page tabloid, was launched by Edward A. Heintz in 1874 in Philadelphia—at that time a major candy manufacturing center. *Confectioners Journal* was acquired by Magazines for Industry, Inc., in 1956 and later merged with *Candy Industry Publication* (founded in 1944, and published as *Candy & Snack Industry* until 1982, when it reverted to its original name, *Candy Industry*). Magazines for Industry, Inc., was acquired by Harcourt Brace Jovanovich, Inc., in 1982.

Medical and pharmaceutical journals first appeared in the late eighteenth and early nineteenth centuries. Among the first was the *Medical Repository*, a quarterly begun in 1797. But it was not until the next century that medical and other professional journals were published in greater numbers. The *New England Journal of Medicine and Surgery*, which continues to this day as the *New England Journal of Medicine*, the official publication of the Massachusetts Medical Society and one of the world's most prestigious publications, was founded in 1812.

Trade Paper Companies

The McGraw-Hill Book Company was among the first major trade paper companies to grow and prosper; it remains the larg-

est business periodical company today (in advertising and subscription revenue).

James H. McGraw and John A. Hill were leaders among a
new breed of progressive trade paper editors and publishers.
They and a number of other journalists believed that the role of
the business press was not only to motivate complacent industries, but to produce editorial products of real value to readers
and advertisers. Successfully incorporating such a philosophy
into the periodicals they produced, McGraw and Hill soon rev-
olutionized the business press. The story of their collaboration
represents one of the major success stories of publishing in the
United States.

James McGraw was a school teacher from upstate New York
who entered the publishing field while in his twenties. In 1888,
at age 28, he acquired control of his first publication, the *American
Journal of Railway Appliances*.

The same year, John Hill, a 30-year-old native of Vermont
and a railroad man who had written articles for *Locomotive Engineer*, left his job with the Denver & Rio Grande Railroad to become
editor of the *Locomotive Engineer*.

McGraw-Hill's beginning dates back to the latter part of the
nineteenth century, an era of explosive industrial expansion, when
large-scale manufacturing, standardization of parts, new machine
tools, and scientific management were beginning to reshape the
nation's economy.

Beginning in the mid-1850s and continuing into the 1880s,
industries discovered that they could no longer be secretive about
their operations. Management had to adapt to new operating
systems, and workers had to be trained fast, instead of undergo-
ing long apprenticeships. This increased the need for communication between industrial firms and their workers. One of management's greatest sources of help in this time of change was the
trade paper or business magazine.

Most trade papers of the early 1880s were "followers" rather
than "leaders" and may be generally characterized as cautious
and fearful of new ideas. But in the mid-1880s, a growing number of trade papers assumed a new leadership stance. Soon trade
papers were founded to serve mechanics, craftsmen, and arti-

sans, in addition to merchants. Because formal specialized education in business was nonexistent at that time, such papers became the "colleges" and "trade schools" of the early period.

The early publishing careers of McGraw and Hill were parallel. The McGraw business developed into a group of trade papers covering the electrical and transportation industries, while Hill built a group of magazines to serve the mechanical and engineering interests of these industries. Both companies also began publishing books.

Since McGraw and Hill were primarily magazine publishers, they left book operations to their respective book-department managers. In 1909, the administrators of these two departments convinced their bosses of the merit of merging the two book operations: The McGraw-Hill Book Company was the result. (The name of the new firm was decided by a flip of a coin, with the winner to have his name first in the title and the loser to become president.) Thus, John Hill was named the company's first president, a position he held until his death in 1916. A year later, Hill's five magazines were merged with the McGraw-Hill Publishing Company, which then became the publisher of 10 business magazines.

The timing of the merger proved fortuitous for the new company, for shortly thereafter, World War I began, inaugurating another period of great industrial growth in the United States. The war accelerated the requirements of factory output and therefore the need for informed managers and engineers. McGraw-Hill's business periodicals responded to the need. At war's end, new industries, including chemicals and aviation, became prominent, and McGraw-Hill and several other publishers launched magazines to serve these and other new fields of business and industry.

Let us now turn briefly to periodicals serving other areas of industry. Beginning in the mid-1850s, several journals were created to serve the growing metal industry. Among the first were the *Hardwaremen's Newspaper; American Manufacturers' Circular*; and the *American Mining Chronical, Iron Manufacturers' and Railway Journal*. (The long title of the latter was needed, it was reasoned, because the publisher wished to explain the full scope of the magazine's contents. Today, a shorter title, perhaps with a sub-title, might be thought more desirable.) These early magazines were the predecessors of today's *Hardware Age* and *Iron Age*, successful publications that continue to change with the industries they serve.

Magazines devoted to the petroleum industry did not assume importance until the latter part of the nineteenth century. One of the first was the *American Gas-Light Journal* (later called the *American Gas Journal*), first published in 1859. Others included *All About Petroleum, National Petroleum Times, Petroleum Gazette and Scientific Journal*, and Hiller's *Petroleum Recorder*.

In addition to McGraw-Hill, Inc., other early trade paper publishers that continue in specialized periodicals today are such stalwarts as the Chilton Book Company (now owned by the American Broadcasting Companies, Inc.), Geyer-McAllister Publications, Petroleum Publishing Company (now PennWell Publishing Company), Bill Communications, Inc., Simmons-Boardman Publishing Corporation, Penton/IPC, Inc. (product of the Penton, Inc., and Industrial Publishing Company merger), Vance Publishing Company, Lebhar Friedman, Inc., Fairchild Publications, Inc. (now owned by Capital Cities Communications, a large, expanding broadcasting and newspaper chain), and the Medical Economics Company, eventually sold to Litton Industries, a California-based, high-technology company. In 1981, Litton sold its Medical Economics Division to International Thomson Organisation Ltd., of London, which controls an important segment of the specialized business press. (See Appendix 4 for a selected listing of multiple business publication publishers.)

Easily the greatest growth area in recent times has been in electronics, and particularly computers. By the end of 1982, there were close to 50 periodicals covering the computer industry, which currently invests nearly $100 million annually in business press advertising and subscriptions. (Total advertising in the specialized business press overall exceeds $2.5 billion annually.) Specific computer periodicals are discussed in later chapters of this book. The point here is that the specialized business press maintains its vitality by being constantly alert to the informational needs of new and developing industries.

Business Journalism in the Daily Press

The first general business newspaper, *The Wall Street Journal*, was founded in 1889; it is today the nation's (and world's) leading business newspaper, boasting the largest daily newspaper circulation in the United States.

While *The Wall Street Journal* is the only general business daily newspaper, the American daily press has always given business some, though often meager, coverage. Today, an increasing number of major urban dailies provide good business coverage. Among the early (now long-defunct) daily newspapers that regularly reported on business were *The New York World, The New York Sun,* and the old *New York Post* (founded in 1882 by Alexander Hamilton and, since the 1940s, a tabloid that publishes a minimum amount of business and financial news).

To better compete with *The Wall Street Journal, The New York Times* became the first general daily newspaper to expand its business news coverage—always of high quality—to a special section, called Business Day and published seven days a week.

Other major dailies in the United States are also moving in this direction: among the most notable of these are *The Boston Globe, The Chicago Tribune, The Chicago Sun Times, The Kansas City Star, The Los Angeles Times, The Washington Post, The Philadelphia Inquirer,* and *The Sun* (Baltimore) (which recently added a special business section), and *The San Francisco Chronicle.* Business coverage in daily newspapers is, in fact, growing phenomenally.

Because of increasing public interest in business news, as well as the expanding coverage in other newspapers, even *The Wall Street Journal* found it desirable to update its format and expand its business coverage. Thus, in 1980, the *Journal* added a second section, in a different format, containing easily comprehended short features on the business scene.

General Business Magazines

The 1970s witnessed tremendous growth in general business magazines intended largely for the general reader interested in keeping in touch with business, as well as for business professionals. (See Chapter 4 for more detailed descriptions of the periodicals mentioned below.)

Business Week, today the flagship periodical of McGraw-Hill Publications Company and the leading general business magazine in the United States, was established in 1929, just before the stock market crash. Started as a monthly entitled *The Magazine of Business* with a circulation of 75,000, *Business Week* in 1982 had an audited circulation of 777,000 and an advertising volume of $133 million. Total revenue for the magazine (including subscriptions) is $160 million, or almost half of McGraw-Hill's $331 million total revenue for its 60 business, technical, and professional publications. The magazine is also responsible for the biggest part ($35 million) of a $61 million operating profit. According to *Folio 400* (September 1981), *Business Week* was fifth in advertising revenue (in 1980) of all magazines, both consumer and trade, the four higher being *Parade, Newsweek, Time*, and *TV Guide*.

The second largest general business magazine is the biweekly, *Forbes*. With a paid circulation of 720,000, it is trying hard to catch up with *Business Week*. It was started by the late B. C. Forbes in 1917, 12 years prior to the founding of *Business Week*. Today, Malcolm S. Forbes, the founder's son, serves as president and editor-in-chief. *Forbes* differs from *Business Week* in that it is more money- and investment-oriented. The style of the magazine also reflects the unique personal touch of Malcolm Forbes, especially in the "Fact and Comment" department.

Fortune, published by Time, Inc., was launched in February 1930, as a monthly—five months after McGraw-Hill had established *The Magazine of Business*. It was *Fortune*'s original intent to publish business-related success stories emphasizing the human element behind the growth of a new corporation. It has changed over the years to become a feature-type general business magazine. From its inception, it has emphasized high-quality graphics and paper and liberal use of color. *Fortune* remained a monthly until 1978, when it was converted to a biweekly to better compete with *Forbes* and *Business Week*. One major modification since its conversion has been the shortening of features, with greater emphasis placed on current business and financial news.

Industry Week, which marked its tenth anniversary in 1980, is published by Penton/IPC, and originated as a conversion from Penton's *Steel*, a long-established weekly periodical. *Industry Week* began life as a weekly (with a guaranteed circulation of 130,000), but within a short time became a biweekly. It now has a circulation of over 300,000 on a controlled basis (i.e., free to select individuals), the only consumer-oriented periodical to be so distributed. Its annual (1981) advertising revenue was $165 million, and it is operating profitably.

Dun's Review, now *Dun's Business Month*, published by Technical Publishing Company, a division of The Dun & Bradstreet Corporation, is a monthly periodical designed for corporate management. Founded in 1893, *Dun's* approach and style changed gradually over the years. In 1981, however, it underwent dramatic alterations, emerging with a new name (*Dun's Business Month*), a different editorial slant, and a new design.

Inc., a magazine for small business company management, was launched in 1979. A paid circulation periodical with over 300,000 subscribers, it has good potential for future growth.

Barron's National Business and Financial Weekly, a weekly tabloid published by Dow Jones & Company, Inc. (owners also of *The Wall Street Journal*), is the nation's leading financial, securities, and investment periodical. Its coverage of the financial scene, while serious and professional, also includes touches of humor, notably in its front page column.

In addition to these leading periodicals, a number of others cover special areas of news. Also, regional and city business periodicals, some in tabloid format, are gaining in prominence. A detailed analysis of this form of business communication is found in Chapter 3.

Statistics of the Business Press

According to *Folio*, a magazine for magazine management (*Folio 400*, September 1982), 161, or 40 percent, of the 400 largest revenue-producing magazines in the United States were specialized business periodicals. The study also showed that of the 10,830 United States magazines in its data base, 5,632 (or 52 percent) were trade publications, while 4,925 (or 49.2 percent) were consumer periodicals.

This means that more business magazines than consumer magazines are now being published in the United States. Also, according to *Folio* (September 1981), the specialized business press accounted for $2.6 billion in total gross revenue, or 24.1 percent of total business press and consumer press revenue, while the smaller number of consumer magazines had $8.2 billion in total gross revenue, or 75.9 percent. This is because the advertising rates of consumer magazines, which boast considerably larger circulations, are much higher than are those of specialized business magazines. In addition, almost all consumer magazines have paid subscriptions, while a greater number of specialized business publications have controlled (or free) circulations. Also, unlike the consumer magazine industry, a much larger portion of overall revenue from specialized business publications comes from the non-*Folio 400* magazines.

Women's Wear Daily (a long-established publication now published by the Fairchild division of Capital Cities Communications) tops *Folio 400*'s list of the 100 largest specialized business periodicals, with annual advertising revenue in excess of $23 million. It is a paid subscription periodical, with annual subscription income of about $4 million.

Second on *Folio 400*'s list is *Computerworld*, a weekly that began in 1967 and has enjoyed phenomenal growth. A news-oriented tabloid, its total revenue is approximately $22 million, not far behind *Women's Wear Daily*. Its greater growth potential than *Women's Wear Daily*, however, makes it likely to become number one in the total trade paper field before long. A description of the magazine's spectacular success is found in Chapter 2.

The remaining eight periodicals in *Folio 400*'s top 10 specialized business periodicals with the largest total revenue are: *Advertising Age, Electronic News, Oil and Gas Journal, Aviation Week & Space Technology, Electronics, Engineering News Record, Machine Design*, and *Electronic Design*, with total revenues ranging from approximately $18 million to $15 million.

The advertising volume of a specialized business magazine depends on the particular industry (or group of industries) it covers. During the late 1970s and the early 1980s, specialized business magazines serving the needs of emerging areas of business and industry have shown the greatest expansion of any period in business press history.

Because some industries reach maturity while others diversify or spin off into new directions, those publishing companies that anticipate emerging and/or changing fields will continue to be more successful than those that follow more conservative publishing approaches.

The areas that have shown the most growth in terms of new periodicals in the last several years have been computers (including word processors); oil exploration; analytical chemistry; and specialized forms of medicine, nursing, and health care. The leading markets in total revenue, according to *Folio 400* (September 1981), have been the computer/original equipment manufacturer (OEM) market, with a growth of 33.7 percent; the electronics market, with a growth of 29.1 percent; and the metal manufacturing market, with a growth of 16.7 percent.

Of the 127 high-revenue-producing specialized business publications identified by *Folio* (1981), 64 are owned by eight large publishing firms. McGraw-Hill, the largest firm, has 17 titles of 127 listed in *Folio*. At latest count, McGraw-Hill owns 30 specialized business magazines and 30 other periodicals, including newsletters and various directories. McGraw-Hill magazines are among the biggest in the industry (in advertising revenue), with a range from $2 million to $25 million per magazine. *Business Week* accounts for almost $150,000 in advertising revenue but it is considered a *general* rather than *specialized* business periodical. The other largest specialized business magazine companies are: Harcourt Brace Jovanovich, Inc.; Technical Publishing Company, a division of Dun & Bradstreet; Cahners Publishing Company, a division of the Reed Holdings of Great Britain; Fairchild Publications, a division of Capital Cities Communications; Penton/IPC, a division of Pittway Corporation; Chilton Company, a division of American Broadcasting Companies; and Communications Channels, Inc., Atlanta, a division of Argus Publishing Co., London. McGraw-Hill, with 1981 annual sales in excess of $1 billion, is the only original company; although a public corporation, it is still substantially owned and managed by the McGraw family. The other companies listed are the result of acquisitions by public corporations not formerly involved in the specialized business press.

About 250 companies, including a growing number of large public corporations, produce approximately 3,000 of the 5,632 specialized business publications. Of these 250, less than half account for 580 audited publications that comprise the membership of the American Business Press, an organization of audited specialized business periodicals and their publishers (discussed at the end of this chapter). The companies range in size from Harcourt Brace Jovanovich, Inc., with 111 business, farm, and professional periodicals, and McGraw-Hill, Inc., with 60 business and professional periodicals, to firms issuing two or three magazines. Many of the larger multi-periodical operations publish between 10 and 20 magazines. Historically, a good percentage of the smaller publishing companies eventually become multi-periodical operations or sell their small, successful magazines to larger firms, because it has become increasingly difficult to publish just one or two magazines profitably over a long period of time. Of course, there are notable exceptions.

Outside the United States, two major multi-media public corporations own and publish about 200 of the 400 or so Canadian business periodicals. About 10,000 specialized business magazines, most of them small (in number of pages per issue and circulation) are published in the rest of the world, with the greatest numbers being from Great Britain, West Germany, Holland, France, the Scandinavian countries, and Japan.

Major Mergers in the Business Press

As a result of the growth and potential of the business press, a trend toward acquisitions and mergers started in the late 1970s and has continued into the early 1980s with no signs of abatement. This trend resembles that experienced by the daily newspapers, but with a difference: Whereas in the newspaper field mergers and acquisitions have occurred within the industry itself, resulting in the formation of major newspaper chains (some of which include television and radio stations, with a handful of publishing magazines), acquisitions of specialized business periodicals have come from outside the field. That is, an increasingly larger number of public communications corporations have acquired specialized business periodicals.

Among the first corporations to enter the business periodical field were Litton Industries, a multi-billion dollar, high-technology corporation that bought into the business press market through the acquisition of the Medical Economics Company (later sold to International Thomson Business Press, the parent of which is International Thomson Organisation, Ltd., of England and Canada); The Times Mirror Company with a medical journal publishing company; and Capital Cities Communications, Inc., which crossed the specialized business publishing threshold in 1967 by purchasing Fairchild Publications, Inc., and has greatly expanded in the years since.

The multi-billion dollar Reed Group of Great Britain now owns the International Publishing Corporation, also of England. The latter, in turn, is the parent of Cahners Publishing Company of Boston, which, since its start with one magazine in the late 1940s, has acquired a representative group of specialized business publishing companies and periodicals to become one of the largest operations in the United States.

Harcourt Brace Jovanovich, Inc. (HBJ), the venerable trade and educational book publishing company, entered the specialized business and professional publishing field in the late 1960s and has since become one of the "big five" in the field. As already mentioned, HBJ is the largest (in number of periodicals) of the specialized business press companies in North America.

Two especially significant mergers took place in 1979: First, the American Broadcasting Companies (ABC) acquired the Chilton Company, a large and long-established publisher in the business press, and one of the few in the field that had also been a public company. Following the Chilton acquisition, ABC bought Ames Publishing Company, publishers of four periodicals, two of which are product news tabloids. The Ames magazines were added to ABC's Chilton division. Several years earlier ABC got its feet wet in business publishing by buying The Miller Publishing Company of Minneapolis and the Hitchcock Publishing

Company of Wheaton, Illinois. Thus, ABC has become a major publisher of specialized business periodicals.

More recently, the Argus Publishing Company of London, a $100 million unit of a large public utility conglomerate, gained a foothold in the U.S. specialized business press through the acquisition (for $13 million cash) of Communications Channels, Inc., Atlanta, Georgia, publisher of more than a dozen business periodicals and one specialized consumer magazine.

Another important merger occurred when Penton merged with Industrial Publishing Company. This gave the latter's parent, the Pittway Corporation (a public industrial corporation), a substantial position in the specialized publishing field.

As still another merger example, The Dun & Bradstreet Corporation (D & B), the multi-billion dollar credit information corporation, which had a number of business and professional magazines, took a giant step by acquiring the Technical Publishing Company in 1977, thus becoming overnight a major business and professional periodical publishing operation. D & B's Technical Publication division has also entered data-base publishing with the acquisition of the Sentry Computer Services, Inc.

One of the latest entrances into specialized business periodical publishing by a major newspaper and magazine company was that of the Hearst Corporation. In August 1980, it acquired the United Technical Publications (UTP) division of Cox Broadcasting Company for $26 million. UTP, with annual sales at the time of acquisition of $22 million, operates about 20 periodicals, the most important of which is the annual *Electronics Engineering Master*, which in 1980 carried 3,712 pages of advertising. UTP publications deal primarily with electronic and allied information services.

Other major communications companies have now begun to follow Hearst's lead, including an increasing number from abroad. For example, International Thomson Organisation Ltd., London, England, and Toronto, Canada, one of the largest publishers of newspapers worldwide, and with other communications enterprises (educational book publishing, legal publishing, microfilm publishing, and academic publishing), has decided to enter business magazine publishing. It formed International

Thomson Business Press (ITBP) for the specific purpose of acquiring and launching periodicals serving various aspects of business and industry. Richard Groves, a former executive of the Chilton Company, has been hired as ITBP's president and chief executive to accomplish the goal of building a major business magazine publishing operation. After initially buying several small periodical operations, Groves took a big step in 1981 by acquiring the Litton Publishing group, including its Medical Economics Division, for an investment of over $85 million.

Charles Mill and the ABP

The observation that people make a business is nowhere more appropriate than in the specialized business press. And no person has done more to promote excellence in specialized business publications and appreciation for their role than Charles Mill, who retired in September 1982 after 10 years as president of The American Business Press, Inc. (ABP), the largest and most prestigious organization of audited specialized business periodicals and their publishers. It is to Charles Mill that I have dedicated this book. Mill, a former publishing executive with Dun-Donnelley Publishing Corporation, a division of Dun & Bradstreet, steered the ABP through some of its years of greatest growth.

As late as the 1960s, the business community and the advertising profession did not regard specialized business magazines or trade papers as vital media. To a large extent, the specialized business press, as an industry, was at fault, having failed to communicate its vitality and indispensability as a communications medium for the business community. Since 1970, this attitude has changed dramatically. We owe this change, to a great extent, to the work of Charles Mill and the ABP.

In an interview with Barbara Love, *Folio* executive editor, in the October 1981 issue of *Folio*, Mr. Mill said:

> "When you consider the complexity of any job in the world today, it is obvious that business publications have an enormously important job to do. Almost all the things the two (political) parties were

talking about during the last [the 1980] election were business matters. Foreign trade, exports, shortages—all those things are business related. And the business press is the primary source of information for those people who are going to solve those problems."

The specialized business press, according to Mill, has also made major contributions to all smaller-circulation magazines, not just business magazines. He explains: "We have been a major force, and in some cases the only force, fighting to make the [U.S.] Postal Service realize the inequalities existing in zone rates. In the most recent postal case, we scored a major victory by keeping down the rates in the farther zones."

The ABP has greatly expanded its list of services in recent years. Currently it publishes 13 monthly newsletters as well as printed matter on numerous subjects of interest to the business press, its readers, and advertisers.

Membership in the ABP is by business magazine company, and periodicals are required to be audited either by the Business Publications Audit (BPA) or the Audit Bureau of Circulations (ABC). The ABP's current membership represents 112 companies that publish 580 periodicals.

The ABP today represents a combination of the original ABP (formed in 1906) and the National Business Publications (NBP) formed in 1940. The original ABP accepted for membership only paid circulation magazines, audited only by the Audit Bureau of Circulations. Because of the growth of controlled circulation, and thus of the Business Publications Audit, however, a separate association, the National Business Publications (NBP), was organized, which accepted for membership periodicals audited by either bureau. As time went on, the NBP surpassed the old ABP in membership. Accordingly, the publishers who belonged to both organizations decided that it would make more sense to combine the two groups into a single professional association. Thus, in 1965, the leaders of the two organizations, with my encouragement, moved to form the new American Business Press, taking the initials of the old ABP but setting up a program combining the best approaches and activities of each.

During the years that followed, the new ABP became a significant force in the growing specialized business magazine business. Its dedicated staff is headed by a salaried president, who is assisted by an executive vice president, vice president, director of information services, and other staff members. It is not a large staff, considering its $1.5 million budget. However, it has been operating efficiently to a large extent because of the contributions of the nonsalaried officers and board of directors, elected from and by the ABP membership.

Following are major ABP functions:

- To provide a wide range of member services, through meetings, seminars, workshops, publication of monthly newsletters and books, folders, and guides.
- To conduct research and marketing activities, thus positioning the business press as a marketing medium.
- To provide a forum for exchanging ideas among publishers of diverse business periodicals.
- To speak for industry concerns as a whole to the federal government.

ABP members are also expected to adhere to its code of publishing practice. Those interested in details of the code, or in information on membership or services, may write or telephone The American Business Press, Inc., 205 E. 42 Street, New York, NY 10017; (212) 661-6360. (See also publications listed at end of Bibliography, Appendix 5.)

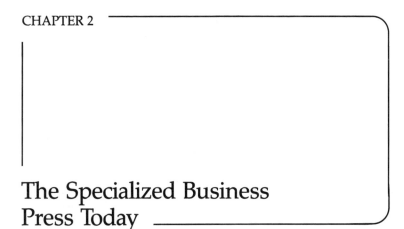

CHAPTER 2

The Specialized Business Press Today

The brief history of specialized business periodicals presented in the first chapter pointed out that the business press has always responded to the development and growth of new and emerging industries and the need for specialized information. Even before an industry matured, a trade paper or specialized business magazine was often launched to serve its communication needs. As the industry matured, other periodicals followed, some directed to more specific facets of the business. This was true, for example, of the food industry, the textile industry, the oil-producing and marketing industry, and the automobile industry, as well as newer fields, including aeronautics, electronics, computer technology, data processing, laser technology, packaging, medical instrumentation, energy-related technology, sound engineering, and electronic data-base publishing.

Today, virtually every industry and profession has one or more magazines devoted to it, and some have a dozen or more catering to special-interest areas. Of the $2.6 billion in advertising that the specialized periodical industry generates, the medical profession claims the largest chunk and also has the largest number of journals—some 350, each covering various medical specialties (including state and regional medical society journals)—with advertising volume of 15 percent, or over $300 million in 1981.

23

Who's Who Among the Publishers

While business magazines may be traced to about the mid-1800s, only two or three surviving magazines and/or firms are 100 years old or older. Periodicals that are 75 years old or older are also few in number, but 50-year old publications are much more common.

As was stated in Chapter 1, most of the growth in business magazine journalism has been in the last 50 years; it accelerated especially following World War II. Those periodicals (and companies) that have survived 75 years or more bear little resemblance to their early beginnings whether in concept, editorial approach, position, and acceptance by the industry or profession they serve, or in the career opportunities they offer.

Among the leading business magazine publishers the following are noteworthy examples:

McGRAW-HILL, INC.

McGraw-Hill, Inc., New York, is the oldest and the largest business magazine publisher; its Publications Division is headed today by John Wrede. While business magazines were McGraw-Hill's original area of concentration, they are no longer its primary products. Today, under the leadership of James H. McGraw, grandson of founder Harold W. McGraw, Jr., McGraw-Hill is a billion dollar-plus public information corporation, involved in almost every area of communications and publishing and a leader in electronic communications and data-base development and marketing.

McGraw-Hill's book and education service unit is now its largest division. Its periodical publishing division, the second largest division, is the company's highest profit maker. This division had advertising and subscription revenue (in 1981) of $331 million and operating profit of $61 million, figures that largely reflect the success of *Business Week*. *Business Week* is by far the largest single product of the division.

McGraw-Hill has acquired more publications than it has launched. Like other publishers (but to a greater degree, largely because of its size, diversity of interest, and high break-even requirement), McGraw-Hill has been forced to sell a large number of its periodicals, most over the last 10 years. These included most of its medical periodicals, such as *Medical World News* (originally a weekly, later changed to biweekly frequency, and for which McGraw-Hill paid over $20 million in stock), *Contemporary Surgery*, and *Contemporary OB/GYN*, as well as its health care periodicals. McGraw-Hill also sold, among others, *Purchasing Week*, *Modern Packaging*, *Merchandising Week*, and *Housing*, and suspended as well its education magazines, at one time leaders in the field. Nevertheless, McGraw-Hill continues as a major force in the business press, fully committed to business periodical publishing as part of its overall information service.

HARCOURT BRACE JOVANOVICH

Harcourt Brace Jovanovich (HBJ), a public corporation whose stock has been traded on the New York Stock Exchange since 1960, is America's largest business, professional, and farm magazine publisher. HBJ has long been a prestigious and financially successful book publishing company. Although its greatest financial achievements have been in the area of textbook publishing, HBJ's reputation also stems from the high-quality books it publishes for the general public. Under the direction of its gifted chairman and chief executive officer William Jovanovich, who started with the company as a salesman over 35 years ago, the business rose to new heights during the 1960s in the number of works published, in the establishment of high standards in publishing, and in diversity of interests.

It was not until 1968 that the company largely entered the specialized business field by acquiring the Ojibway Press of Duluth, Minnesota, for $6.5 million in HBJ stock. Marshall Reining and Robert Edgell, the principals of Ojibway, left the company shortly after the merger.

Inasmuch as HBJ had made a commitment to expand its business magazine publishing operations, in 1970 it brought back Robert Edgell from his "early retirement" and installed him as general manager of the business magazine division, with the directive to build a large, profitable, and forward-looking business magazine operation. Edgell is now chairman and chief executive officer of HBJ's Communications and Services, Inc., one of HBJ's three main operating companies. He is director of the parent corporation and a member of HBJ's Office of the President, and he has enabled HBJ's business magazine division to expand to its present size.

How did Edgell do this? By spinning off (through sale or discontinuance) some of the lesser Ojibway publications; by merging those periodicals with greater growth potential with larger, newly acquired magazines; and, most important, by launching a campaign to buy business and professional magazines that were seasoned and had major market positions with still greater growth potential. The business magazine field is generally an industry of entrepreneurs. Edgell is an entrepreneur who is also a professional manager.

A representative number of the 111 business, professional, and farm periodicals that HBJ now owns (including the 16 Magazines For Industry, Inc., titles acquired in 1982) have important market positions in health care, energy, agriculture, education, merchandising, food service and processing, communications, and travel and lodging. One of HBJ's notable successes is *Food Management,* a personal creation of Mr. Edgell's. A combination of several food service periodicals, *Food Management* has been converted to a high-quality publication covering the food service field for hospitals, schools, and other institutions.

Among HBJ's most respected (and larger advertising volume) magazines are those in the medical field. Edgell is credited with a coup of sorts in HBJ's 1976 acquisition of the *Modern Medicine* group of publications from The New York Times Company for about $6.5 million in cash. Among the journals in the group are *Modern Medicine, U.S.A.,* and its licensed foreign counterparts. The foreign units of *Modern Medicine* generate significant profits. Today, *Modern Medicine* is one of the most successful periodicals in the field of medical journalism. It is highly profitable and continues to grow. The HBJ health care group also includes magazines such as *Geriatrics, Neurology, Physician's Management, Dental Management,* and *Hospital Formulary.*

Instructor is the leading magazine in the field of elementary school education. In the merchandising area HBJ magazines in the fashion, home, housewares, toys, and hobby fields are major enterprises. *Communication News* leads several magazines in its field, as does *Food & Drug Packaging.*

HBJ's farm magazines cover 10 states and are part of the acquisition of the Harvest Publishing Company. Five of these magazines were founded more than a century ago. HBJ also has newsletters in aviation, cosmetics, and real estate.

Of the 8,200 HBJ employees, almost 1,500 are involved in the specialized business press centered in Duluth, where circulation, production, accounting, and art departments are located, and in one of the headquarters of HBJ, Inc., in Cleveland. Sales offices are located at 747 Third Avenue and at 111 Fifth Avenue, New York.

MAGAZINES FOR INDUSTRY, INC.
(NOW PART OF HBJ PUBLICATIONS)

The substantial entrance of large public corporations into the business press area through major acquisitions will not spell the end of the entrepreneurs. While it will undoubtedly cost more in the future to launch a new magazine, creative magazine editors with a business bent and a desire for ownership will continue to try their luck with new business periodicals.

The "down-side" risk in starting a business periodical is not great, certainly not when compared to starting a new consumer periodical or a business involved in producing and marketing a line of products. And though the potential for profit may not be as great as that of a high-technology company, for example, the rewards, both in personal fulfillment and in dollars, can be substantial.

After the success of the initial periodical, there is no reason, moreover, not to start a second and later a third magazine, using profits from the first venture to finance the other two. In this manner, multi-publication business periodical companies have been formed and will continue to be formed—something for the business magazine journalist to contemplate as he or she begins a career.

My own experience is a case in point. I began my career as an assistant editor on a weekly food magazine and within a few months was promoted to associate editor. After a year I moved to another company, becoming associate editor of another food weekly. In less than two years I became editor of the magazine. After about a dozen years as editor of two different magazines, and with a great desire to own a business magazine or at least part of one, I left a well-paying position as editor and publisher of a weekly food periodical and launched a biweekly, tabloid-style periodical serving one of the industries covered by the magazine on which I had been employed. I started with $6,000; subscriptions, many with checks, began to come in almost immediately after I mailed the first announcement. At the same time, I was successful in selling enough advertising to break even with the first issue and several subsequent issues and wound up the first year with a small profit. I credit my initial success largely to my experience as editor and publisher through which I had developed a following and a credibility in the industry covered by the new magazine.

The first magazine was started in 1944; it was followed by a second in 1946 and a third in 1959. Each new periodical was launched on the successes of the previous one, enabling me to utilize the available profits and cash flow. Today the company I started, Magazines For Industry, Inc., comprises seven specialized business magazines and nine other publishing properties, including a technical book publishing operation, and annually grosses close to $9 million. It is now part of HBJ Publications, a large and expanding division of Harcourt Brace Jovanovich, Inc.

THE AMERICAN BROADCASTING COMPANIES, INC. (ABC)

ABC entered the specialized business publications field in the late 1970s (the only one of the three national broadcasting firms to do so to date) by acquiring two medium-size but long-established companies: Miller Publishing Company of Minneapolis, Minnesota, and shortly thereafter the Hitchcock Publishing Company of Wheaton, Illinois.

Before the end of the 1970s ABC bought the large and venerable Chilton Company of Radnor, Pennsylvania, and soon afterward acquired the Ames Publishing Company, Philadelphia, publisher of several product tabloid periodicals.

Chilton, with over thirty specialized business magazines, including several large magazines such as *Iron Age* and *Food Engineering*, put ABC among the leading business magazine publishers. While the profitability of the business press could not match that of broadcasting, ABC decided that this communications area offered substantial growth potential, and it has plans to acquire other business magazine properties.

Chilton's history dates back to 1911, when the company was chartered in Delaware under the name of the United Publishers Corporation. Originally called the Chilton Class Journal Company, the firm was acquired by United in 1923, and in 1934, the combined business was changed to the Chilton Company.

Indirectly, Chilton traces its origin to 1899, when the late George Buzby, along with the late James C. Artman and the late C. A. Musselman, founded Chilton's and United's predecessor company, known as the Trade Publishing Company. George's son, Carroll, served as president and later chairman of Chilton from 1955 until his death in 1970. As the successor to Joseph H. Hildreth, Carroll Buzby was an outstanding leader in the business magazine industry.

Though Chilton had for years been a public corporation (its stock was traded over the counter), controlling interest in the company had long been in the hands of the Pew family of Sun Oil (Sonoco). This arrangement changed following the deaths of several members of the Pew family, but 45 percent of the company's stock remained in the control of the Pew-organized Glenmede Trust Company of Philadelphia until April 1979, when the stock was sold to the American Broadcasting Companies. ABC then acquired all other available stock—at $86 per share—for a total investment of about $50 million.

Chilton is a totally integrated company. It owns its own modern headquarters building, designed and built specifically for Chilton in 1970, in Radnor, Pennsylvania. It is also one of the few business magazine companies that owns its own printing and typesetting facilities, a fully integrated computer setup, and a research department.

Chilton's sales in 1978 (the last full year prior to its acquisition by ABC) totaled $72,396,312, with net profits after taxes of $3,363,011. While its business periodical volume and earnings have grown over the years, the percentage of total sales in this area has declined, largely because of Chilton's expansion into other fields. Thus, in 1977, its industrial periodical business accounted for 53 percent of the company's total volume of almost $65 million, compared to 77.5 percent of the company's total volume of just over $20 million in 1963.

A number of Chilton's periodicals are leaders in their fields, boasting an annual advertising volume in the multi-millions. Chilton is the leader (by far) in the automotive field, with such magazines as *Automotive Industries, Commercial Car Journal, Automotive Marketing, Fleet Specialist, Motor Age, Owner Operator*, and *Automotive Industries International*. During the recent economic problems in the automobile industry, however, Chilton's automotive publications suffered declines in advertising pages and revenue.

Other sizable Chilton business magazines are *Food Engineering, Hardware Age, Iron Age*, and *Product Design & Development*. Chilton also has an important book company, and is a leader in automotive books.

Chilton also has interest (with McGraw-Hill, Inc.) in a paper mill and in real estate (with mineral rights).

William A. Barbour was Chilton's president and chief executive officer from 1972 until September 1982, at which time he retired and was replaced as president by Gary R. Ingersoll, former manager of International Telephone & Telegraph (ITT) Corporation's Technical Education and Training Division, who in turn was replaced by Lawrence A. Fornasieri, formerly a vice president and chief financial officer at the Educational and Professional Publishing division of CBS, Inc.

Barbour represents an excellent example of a successful career in business journalism. With a bachelor's degree in journalism from Montana State University, he joined Chilton in 1952, holding various jobs including editorial assistant, editor, publisher, and publishing vice president before becoming chief executive officer of the company.

The Miller Publishing Company, ABC's first acquisition in the business press, dates back to 1873 when it launched *The Northwestern Miller*, thus becoming one of the first business magazine publishing firms in the United States. *The Northwestern Miller* became the leading publication of the international milling trade. But times change, and in the year of its centennial, 1973, *The Northwestern Miller* published its final issue.

Why did Miller Publishing decide to retire its first periodical? Simply because the magazine could no longer be positioned in the changing marketplace. By 1973, the milling industry had changed so dramatically that there had ceased to be a need for a magazine to provide specific information for millers. In fact, at the time that the magazine stopped publication, it was directed more to the cereal industry, which had absorbed the milling field over the years. But even this change in audience had not been enough to ensure the publication's continued vitality.

Thus, a crucial fact of business is again demonstrated: The business press, like the industries it serves, is a volatile, constantly changing field that must respond to the ebb and flow of consumer demands. Only by adjusting to new technological and marketing concepts and developments (that in turn create new types of industries and sometimes new business fields altogether) can publications keep abreast of the industries they serve. This means that managers of business magazine publishing companies—and particularly editors—must continually anticipate upcoming technological and marketing innovations, often months and sometimes years before they actually occur. Sometimes changes are so dramatic that the best response is to create a wholly new publication.

This is exactly what the Miller Publishing Company has done. Today, 12 of Miller's 15 business magazine titles are less than 25 years old, with some much younger. Miller continues to be largely involved in "agri-" (or agricultural) publishing. Its primary publication is *Feedstuffs*, a weekly, news-oriented tabloid serving agribusiness. Originally a spin-off of a section in *The Northwestern Miller* (in 1929), it now serves over 20,000 managers (in the United

States and 75 foreign countries) involved in livestock and poultry feed, feeding, and marketing industries. It also publishes an annual compendium of the total feedstuffs industry. Other periodicals published by Miller include *Feedlot Management, Hog Farm Management, Dairy Herd Management, Farm Store Merchandising*, and the *Home and Garden Supply Merchandiser*. The company provides, as well, a number of ancillary services such as the Miller Agricultural Research Services and Agrimail (for direct mail marketing).

Now, as part of the large and growing business press division of ABC, Miller continues to be headed by Wilfred E. Lingren as president. Lingren, in his late fifties, has served as an accomplished spokesperson both in industries covered by the company's periodicals and in the business press, where he has been a member of the board of directors and chairman of the American Business Press.

BILLBOARD PUBLICATIONS, INC.

An interesting example of the growth of a periodical and its company is found in Billboard Publications, Inc., New York, headed by William Donaldson Littleford as chairman and chief executive officer. The grandson of the founder of *Billboard* magazine, Littleford is a leader in the billboard industry and a well-known personality in business magazine publishing.

Billboard began life in 1894 as a monthly called *Billboard Advertising*. Its founder was William H. Donaldson, who formed a partnership with James F. Hennegan. Both Donaldson and Hennegan worked in the Donaldson's family firm, which specialized in printing bill posters for traveling shows. William Donaldson reasoned that people in show business, who were home only a few months of the year at best, would appreciate a publication that kept them in touch with activities in show business and with one another. He reasoned correctly.

Billboard Advertising, which made its debut in 1894, carried the slogan: "A monthly resume of all that is new, bright, and interesting on the boards." The first issue was eight pages long and sold for 10 cents a copy (90 cents for a year's subscription).

From this modest beginning, *Billboard* developed into a multi-million dollar weekly news-oriented magazine from which were spun off other entertainment-related informational media and magazines, so that today, Billboard Publications, Inc., is one of the larger and more prosperous business magazine companies.

Over the years, as *Billboard* changed from monthly to weekly frequency, its editorial objectives and coverage also changed. The magazine at one time covered all facets of the amusement industry, but in the late forties it began to specialize in the burgeoning music and recording business industries (it thus represents another example of a business magazine in the forefront of industrial change). This specialization culminated in the splitting of the magazine into two periodicals, *Billboard* and *Amusement Business*, in 1960. *Billboard* since then has served only the music/record industries and has grown substantially, becoming the undisputed leader in the field. Although *Amusement Business* initially experienced more than its share of growing pains, once it found its proper position in the marketplace, it too began to prosper and today brings in over $1.5 million in revenue.

In addition to *Billboard, Amusement Industry*, and a number of other entertainment periodicals, Billboard Publications now owns *The American Artist* and *Photo Weekly* and operates as well *The American Artist Book Club*. Its business is international in scope. Several years ago, Billboard sold two specialized consumer magazines to Columbia Broadcasting Systems (CBS) in order to settle an estate, thus making it almost exclusively a business magazine publisher, with much growth potential.

SIMMONS-BOARDMAN PUBLISHING CORPORATION

Simmons-Boardman is another veteran in business magazine publishing, its first magazine, *Western Railroad Gazette*, dating back to 1856. In 1876, *Western Railroad Gazette* and several other railway periodicals were combined to become *Railway Age*, which became the company's leading periodical.

Simmons-Boardman itself was incorporated on October 3, 1883, with headquarters in New York. The company has experienced its share of ups and downs over the years, largely because of the upheavals in the railway industry (still the company's primary involvement). The company has also undergone several different ownerships. Today its principal stockholder and chief executive officer is Arthur J. McGinnis, who is also chairman of the executive committee. Under his direction, Simmons-Boardman has fared well, generating almost $10 million in annual revenue (in 1981).

In addition to the biweekly *Railway Age* (it was a weekly until recently) and a number of other railroad periodicals, Simmons-Boardman publishes *Marine Engineering/Log* and several reference periodicals, including *Plant Location, Car & Locomotive Cyclopedia,* and *Who's Who in Railroading.* It also publishes *The Journal of the American Bankers Association,* on contract with that trade group, and *Columbia Today,* the Columbia University alumni periodical. The company also has a book division and provides information and training services in railroading, as well as a direct mail service in railroading and the maritime industries.

GORDON PUBLICATIONS, INC.

Gordon Publications, Inc., Morristown, New Jersey, founded by Theodore Gordon in 1962, is unique in that it publishes only product tabloids—eighteen 11-by-16-inch tabloid-style periodicals that together comprise, in the words of the company's director of marketing, a "giant that looks and reads like a Sears catalog."

Gordon is not the first to publish product tabloids but he (and his associates) have developed this type of periodical into a kind of art form. Gordon created each of his tabloids to cover a different industry or field of interest, including several new and upcoming industries. Among the tabloid titles are: *Biomedical Products, Solar Heating & Cooling, Computer Products, Computer Dealer, Chemical Equipment, Laboratory Equipment, Mining/Processing Equipment, Petrochemical Equipment News, Purchasing Digest, Heating & Plumbing Merchandiser,* and *Surgical Product News.* Gordon has introduced one magazine a year on the average. By the time this book is published, there will likely be one to three new Gordon tabloids.

What distinguishes a product tabloid from all other specialized business periodicals is that it has one paramount purpose—to produce inquiries for advertisers (and the companies whose products are covered in the tabloid's editorial content). The inquiries are in the form of specially designed cards, featured in each issue of a tabloid, that readers fill out and mail to the publisher. Although the traditional specialized business magazine offers its readers a variety of reading material—news stories, features, interviews, market trends, technological developments, product news, and more—the product tabloid contains only news and advertisements of new products. Image building for industry is clearly not its function.

With some exceptions, the typical reader of product tabloids and the person who normally fills out the inquiry cards is the middle manager. Does business result from such inquiry cards? The answer is yes, despite the fact that many cards are sent by readers solely for the purpose of receiving product information. Some corporations actually frown on the inquiry card because of the cost involved in the "follow-through" and the minimal return they have received. Such firms have thus refused to have their new products included in the product tabloids. They represent a small minority, however. Most corporations like to receive inquiry cards even though only a handful received are normally found useful.

BILL COMMUNICATIONS, INC.

Bill Communications is one of the oldest business magazine companies, founded in 1879 by Colonel Edward Lyman Bill and his cousin, Jefferson Davis Bill. Their first periodical was called *Music Trade Review*. Jefferson Bill remained with the company for only ten years, retiring in 1889. Colonel Bill then took over the operation, bringing his two sons, Raymond and Edward, into the management team. They eventually succeeded him. Following their deaths in the mid-1950s, Bill Brothers Publications, Inc., as it was then named, continued to operate under the existing management, following the brothers' expressed wish. Today, after years of sluggish growth, the company is a large New York-based magazine operation, with annual revenue exceeding $35 million. It is employee-owned under a program of ESOT, but continues to have a family connection. Chairman and major stockholder of Bill Communications is John Hartman, who is married to Esther Kelly Bill, a daughter of the late Raymond Bill. Hartman, now in his fifties, joined the company in 1949 as a salesperson on *Sales Management*. He served the company in various capacities—largely in sales—before becoming executive vice president, and then president in 1957. It was more than a decade later, however, before Bill Communications experienced notable growth. In a 1970 case study for the Harvard Business School, Hartman did not hesitate to state:

> "Ten years ago Bill Communications was a slowly dying company. Years as a family run business had left it low on cash, unable to make acquisitions. With a general climate not conducive to growth, it had only one really first-rate magazine, *Sales Management*. The others were simply going nowhere in particular, since they were not leaders in their various markets."

How Bill Communications grew to become an exciting and profitable company, with revenues raised from under $4 million in 1958 to more than $35 million today, makes an instructive story.

Except for the largest, business magazine companies usually remain single-product fields, confining their business to publishing and making no serious attempt to get involved in allied operations. Bill Communications proceeded differently. In an effort to strengthen the company, it decided to take two steps: first, to improve and enlarge its business magazine periodicals; and second, to expand, as well, into peripheral product and service areas. The latter included formation of an Information Division to include books and directories, market statistics, a data bank, plus seminars and other services.

Diversification helped to increase the company's profit volume. The effort to improve the profitability of the company's magazines was assigned to Donald Karas, senior vice president of the corporation. Under his direction, *Fast Foods* grew substantially. A companion publication called *Institutional Distribution* and, later, *Dining*, were also introduced. Eventually, *Dining* was merged with *Fast Foods* to become *Restaurant Business*.

Plastics Technology, another of the company's publications, which had not grown appreciably over the years, was improved markedly, and its advertising volume followed suit. The periodical is now a leader in its field. *Sales Management* was also expanded to include marketing content, and the magazine's title was changed to *Sales and Marketing Management*. This change proved helpful in increasing acceptance and advertising volume.

The corporate structure was also changed. The new structure called for instituting a "bottoms up or participative management" philosophy. Based on the business philosophy of Chairman John Hartman, this called for greater responsibility for divisional managers and line executives.

Hartman now involves himself in company affairs only part-time. President and operating chief is Morgan Browne, former executive vice president. Browne came to Bill Communications in 1956 when the company acquired *Tide* magazine from Billboard Publications (Browne was then *Tide*'s editor). Though the magazine was sold three years later, Browne remained at Bill Communications and was instrumental in its growth. Editorially oriented, Browne is a self-educated generalist and an expert in business magazine publishing. He has no formal college education, and started his career at *Tide* without prior journalistic training. His is an exceptional case of "learning while doing" and one that could probably not be duplicated today.

GRALLA PUBLICATIONS

Gralla Publications, New York, is one of the younger, more successful business magazine companies. Starting in 1951, brothers Lawrence and Milton Gralla operated the Nationwide Trade News Service Corporation—a service for business magazines similar to that provided for newspapers by the Associated Press and the United Press. Before long, Nationwide Trade News Service provided news and handled assignments for more than 200 magazines.

The Grallas soon decided, however, to become business magazine publishers themselves, having found that there was no periodical covering the growing kitchen business area. Thus, in 1955, they launched *Kitchen Business*, now called *Kitchen and Bath Business*. It was an instant success.

Today, Gralla publishes 15 periodicals, most of them in tabloid form. In addition, Gralla publishes directories and also owns and manages eight national and international trade shows. The magazines started by Gralla, in addition to *Kitchen and Bath Business*, are: *Bank Systems & Equipment, Sporting Goods Business, Catalog Showroom Business, Meeting News, Contract, Premium/Incentive Business, National Jeweler, Health Care Products News, Facilities Design and Management, Giftware Business, Merchandising, Multi-Housing News, Travel Agent Marketplace*, and *Impressions*.

The Gralla brothers have been as successful with magazines they acquired as with those they started. A good example is the *National Jeweler*. When they took over control in 1971, it was a small, mediocre publication. Today, it is not only one of Gralla's largest, but also one of the most important periodicals in the entire business magazine industry.

The Gralla Company is a $40-million-plus business with much growth ahead. The company is headed by the two Gralla brothers. Lawrence, the younger is president, and Milton is executive vice president. Both are editorially oriented, but Lawrence appears to have a stronger feeling for finance, while Milton is the editorial chief. The attitude expressed by Lawrence is a key factor in the company's success—and a prime ingredient in any successful business magazine company: "We just do not publish and mail a magazine. We become part of the industry the magazine services."

Industry involvement is, indeed, crucial and is a major feature distinguishing business magazines from consumer publications. In the Gralla brothers' case, the most interesting example of their success is found in their company's involvement with the apartment construction business. "We felt that the association covering this industry was not doing its job for the industry," said Milton. "The absence of a well-done trade show was hurting the industry and consequently our magazine, *Apartment Construction News*. So in 1969 we started a trade show." The trade show has been highly successful. It not only added profitable volume to the Gralla company, but actually made *Apartment Construction News* bigger and more profitable.

In the late summer of 1983, United Newspapers of London, publishers of 60 daily newspapers and magazines, including the *Yorkshire Post* and *Punch*, acquired Gralla Publications for $44 million. President Lawrence Gralla and Executive Vice President Milton Gralla will continue to head up the operation, which is expected to acquire other specialized newspapers and magazines.

United is the fourth British publishing company to have entered the American specialized business press through acquisition. The others are Argus Publishing Company of London, IPC/Reed Holdings, and Thomson Ltd.

TECHNICAL PUBLISHING COMPANY

Easily one of the most successful business magazine companies, and one that experienced record growth in the 1970s, is the Technical Publishing Company, Great Barrington, Illinois, now part of the Dun & Bradstreet Corporation (D & B).

With the possible exception of CW Communications, Inc., publishers of the successful weekly tabloid *Computerworld*, Technical Publishing has enjoyed the most spectacular growth record of any business magazine operation. Though the company was incorporated in March 1960, by Edward R. Shaw, Arthur L. Rice, Sr., and Charles S. Clarke, it had remained a small, family-owned company until 1969 when it went public and launched its meteoric expansion program. In 1964, its business consisted largely of publishing two magazines, *Power Engineering* and *Plant Engineering*. At that time, Technical Publishing had 77 employees, a sales volume of just over $2 million, and net profits of only $52,000. By the end of 1975, the company employed 300 personnel, reported sales of $21 million, and net earnings of $1,475,000. For 1976, revenue reached $26 million and net profits a record $2,777,000. With net profits better than 10 percent of sales, it was one of the most lucrative companies in the industry.

In 1978 Technical Publishing Company sold its business to Dun & Bradstreet. At that time it published eight business magazines: *Consulting Engineer, Datamation, Pollution Engineering, Electric Light and Power, Purchasing World, Research Development, Power Engineering,* and *Plant Engineering.*

Today the new Technical Publishing Company, as a division of Dun & Bradstreet, also includes the magazines originally owned by Dun-Donnelley Publishing Corporation, a division of Dun & Bradstreet. These are: *Dun's Business Month, American Journal of Cardiology, American Journal of Medicine, American Journal of Surgery, Consulting Engineer, Control Engineering, Cutis, Datamation, Electric Light & Power, Fire Engineering, Graphic Arts Monthly, Highway and Heavy Construction, Industrial Research/Development, Mining Equipment International, Plant Engineering, Pollution Engineering, Power Engineering, Purchasing World, Water and Wastes Engineering, World Construction,* and *Computer Product News.*

Technical Publishing also produces catalogs and directories and is involved in consumer-oriented books (Technical acquired DBI Books in 1975). In addition, it has an education and training systems program now involving over 12,000 industrial plants, utilities, hospitals, and government facilities, and a long list of other business-oriented services. It also publishes specialized consumer magazines.

The spark plug behind the new growth program was and continues to be James B. Tafel, former chairman and chief executive. In March 1983, Mr. Tafel retired from the Technical post, at which time Technical's president, Jack Abely, Dun-Donnelly's former operating chief, assumed the chairmanship.

When Tafel became executive vice president and assumed the company's future development program in 1966, he took up the task of realizing two goals: to go public and to acquire additional magazines and other businesses for Technical. Within a year, Tafel had positioned the company in both directions. In 1969, Technical Publishing went public. It was one of the best of times to accomplish this objective, since it proved to be the peak of the big years of mergers, acquisitions, and going public, trends that were to cease the following year, not to be resumed until the mid-1970s. As of 1982, no other business periodical company had gone public since the mid-1970s.

Other companies publish considerably more magazines than does Technical, but none, with the exception of McGraw-Hill, has as many large (in advertising revenue) magazines. Publication size has proved to be an important factor in the company's growth. In the business magazine field success or failure is often determined by the type of magazines published, the size of the markets covered, and the growth potential of each publication. The seven original periodicals published by Technical (exclusive of those added through the merger with Dun & Bradstreet) serve large, established markets with measurable growth potential. In the business magazine field, it has become increasingly difficult to turn much of a profit unless a magazine has $1 million minimum in annual advertising revenue (except for the small, one- or two-publication owners who do most of the work themselves). Obviously, the bigger the advertising volume, the better. The most successful companies are those owning several magazines, each with many millions of dollars in advertising revenue. Each of Technical's seven is a multi-million dollar periodical and each has continued to grow.

Because the management of Technical, under Tafel's leadership, was hungry for accelerated growth—its long-range objective was to become the preeminent business and technical magazine publishing company—it took a step in midsummer 1977 that caught many companies by surprise. It moved to merge with Dun-Donnelley Publishing Corporation, a subsidiary of The Dun & Bradstreet Corporation. When finally completed, before the end of 1977, the merger proved to be a $45 million transaction (the Technical stockholders received that much in D & B stock). While the merger with Dun-Donnelley brought Technical Publishing under the parent ownership of D & B, the new, combined publishing operation continues to be known as Technical Publishing Company and its headquarters remains in Great Barrington.

What are the implications of the merger for Dun & Bradstreet and for the business press community in general? In terms of financial capability, it means that the combined business magazine operation will have access to a great deal more financial clout, since parent Dun & Bradstreet has annual volume in excess of $1 billion, with net profits in excess of $100 million and substantial working capital. Thus, today Dun & Bradstreet as a public corporation is slightly bigger than McGraw-Hill, Inc., as well as most of the other public companies that own business magazines. Its total publishing business, which includes telephone directories, amounts to over $400 million.

From the viewpoint of the business magazine community, the Technical/Dun & Bradstreet merger, and the already mentioned Chilton-ABC merger, signaled a trend whereby large listed public companies were moving to buy medium-size business and professional magazine companies. Such a trend could have obvious significance for the viability of medium-size business publishers. It could also mean the entrance into ancillary fields by the larger and medium-size business and professional magazine companies.

PENTON/IPC, INC.

The 1976 merger of Penton, Inc., and the Industrial Publishing Company (IPC), both of Cleveland, now called Penton/IPC, created another of the largest business magazine publishing operations in this country. IPC was, and now Penton/IPC is, a subsidiary of Pittway Corporation, the Chicago-based public company (listed on the American Stock Exchange). Pittway paid Penton stockholders $18 million for the operation. Thomas L. Dempsey, president of IPC and a vice president of Pittway, became chairman and chief executive officer of the combined Penton/IPC, while Sal F. Marino, president and chief executive officer of Penton, Inc. became president of the combined Penton/IPC. Pittway, headed by Nelson Harris, has interests in fire and burglar alarm systems and aerosol packaging, in addition to business and professional communications.

Penton, the larger of the two publishing companies, had annual sales in 1975 of $45 million, while IPC's sales in that year amounted to $25 million. Penton publishes six specialized magazines, including the large and successful *Machine Design*, which has annual advertising revenue in excess of $12 million; *New Equipment Digest*, with annual advertising volume in excess of $7 million; and the biweekly *Industry Week* (an outgrowth of the weekly, *Steel*), with annual revenue in excess of $12 million. Penton also owns and operates a printing plant in Cleveland, and offers education and other ancillary services.

IPC's periodicals were small (in advertising revenue) compared to Penton's. Of IPC's 13 monthly magazines, the largest are *Government Product News*, with an annual volume of about $2.5 million, *Modern Office Procedures*, with annual revenue slightly below that, and *Handling & Shipping*, with annual volume of about $2 million. IPC also publishes four bienniel directories and is involved in a number of marketing communication activities.

The combined Penton/IPC business now includes 25 magazines, a number of directories, a printing plant, and ancillary services including trade shows, seminars, correspondence courses, and telephone and mail marketing services. As part of a growing public company, Penton/IPC is now in a position to acquire other business and professional magazines, to expand its ancillary operation, and to enter new communication fields. As of 1981, the combined revenue of Penton/IPC exceeded $150 million.

Penton, the older of the two companies, was incorporated in 1904 in Ohio and is a successor to The Foundry Publishing Company, established by the late John A. Penton in 1892. Its first magazine was *Foundry*, now called *Foundry Management & Technology*. In 1968, the company was reincorporated in Delaware, and in 1975 its corporate name was changed to Penton, Inc. Its stock was traded over the counter. Until his retirement in the early 1970s, Russ Jahnke, who was first the company's president and later its chairman and chief executive officer, played a major role in the development of the Penton business. A good manager, he surrounded himself with excellent professional talent, including Sal F. Marino, a creative, promotion- and marketing-oriented publishing executive who succeeded Jahnke as president and chief executive officer.

Penton/IPC now employs approximately 1,000 people in its various businesses, including 150 editors, most of whom are not only professional business journalists but also have expertise in the fields covered by their magazines.

GEYER-McALLISTER PUBLICATIONS, INC.

An interesting and in some respects unusual company in business magazine publishing is Geyer-McAllister Publications, Inc., of

New York. A medium-size operation with annual volume (in 1982) in excess of $8 million, Geyer-McAllister is exceptional in that since its founding, over 100 years ago, it has always been owned, in part, by the same family. The company is all the more remarkable in that the magazine it launched in 1877 is still published today, though under a different name.

The story of Geyer-McAllister begins with Andrew Geyer. In April 1877, after several years of working in the stationery field and as an employee in trade papers, he published his first magazine, *Geyer's Stationer*, the predecessor of today's *Geyer's Dealer Topics*. The new magazine, published twice monthly, was initially 20 pages, eight of which were advertising, and had an introductory circulation of 2,000. Within three months, the size of the issue doubled. In the years following, the magazine continued to grow with the expanding stationery industry, of which publisher Geyer was a leading figure. *Geyer's Stationer* eventually did so well that in 1895 it became a weekly, with news and features on the latest merchandising techniques, display ideas, and new products, thus setting the pace for other business magazines.

Geyer-McAllister is one of the very few specialized business periodical publishing companies whose magazines continue on an all paid subscription basis, thus opposing current trends toward controlled (free) circulation.

Geyer's Stationer was only one of Andrew Geyer's successes. He also introduced *Geyer's Lists*, which later became *Geyer's Reference Directory* and was eventually changed to *Geyer's Who Makes It and Where*. The publication is still published today as *Geyer's Who Makes It*, the buying guide of the industry.

Following Geyer's death in 1919, his widow, Mary A. Geyer, assumed management of the operation, and in so doing became one of the first women to run a business magazine publishing company. She continued active until a few years before her death in 1965. By that time, her nephew, Donald McAllister, who joined the company in the early 1920s, was president. (The company's name had also been changed to Andrew Geyer-McAllister, Inc.) McAllister, now eighty (in 1982) continues to run the company, Geyer-McAllister Publications, Inc., as chairman and chief executive officer.

In addition to *Geyer Dealer Topics*, now a monthly, Geyer-McAllister publishes four other monthly magazines—*Administrative Management, Word Processing World, Gifts & Decorative Accessories*, and *Playthings*—as well as newsletters and directories.

Editorially oriented, chairman Donald McAllister has encouraged his editors to develop business journalism as a career, including participation in management. Solid editorial training, in his opinion, is a valuable asset in management—whether as publisher, president, or chairman of a company. (A good case in point at Geyer-McAllister is the career of George Tice, who rose through the editorial ranks of the company to become publisher of *Geyer's Dealer Topics* and vice president of the corporation.)

Donald McAllister launched his career as an editorial trainee following graduation from Cornell University in 1922, and moved up in the company until he became publisher and, eventually, chief executive. (His son, Donald, Jr., after graduating from the Medill School of Journalism of Northwestern University in 1972, joined the editorial staff of the company and has grown with it, too).

CRAIN COMMUNICATIONS, INC.

Crain Communications, Inc., of Chicago, entered the specialized business periodical world with Volume 1, Number 1 of *Advertising Age*, on January 11, 1930, at the start of the Great Depression. (On January 7, 1980, the magazine celebrated its fiftieth anniversary.) *Advertising Age* was initially a 12-page, weekly tabloid (five-column) that called itself *"The National Newspaper of Advertising."* Its founder, and the president and publisher of Crain Communications, was G. D. Crain, Jr.

G. D. Crain (he was always called G. D.; his full name never appeared in *Ad Age*) was a newsman from the beginning of his career. But he was equally committed to owning his own publishing business. Born in Louisville, Kentucky, he graduated from the Louisville Male High School, where he was an editor of the school paper. He received a scholarship to Centre College, Danville, Kentucky, where, in three years he received both a bachelor of arts and a master of arts degree. His first journalism job was as a reporter for the *Louisville Herald,* and at age 21, he became city editor of the *Herald.* Crain launched his publishing business following a stint at starting and running a freelance editorial service. His first magazine, in 1916, was *Hospital Management,* followed one month later by a second called *Class,* later changed to *Industrial Marketing.* Shortly thereafter, Crain moved the business from Louisville to Chicago.

Crain's principal competitor there was the flourishing Printers Ink Publishing Company, which published two periodicals for the communications field—a standard-size monthly magazine and a "digest"-size news weekly, consisting largely of short news items about advertising. The monthly was a feature-type publication. Crain felt that *Printers Ink,* while an important medium of communications, was too feature-oriented and was not providing the simple, direct news that he believed the advertising profession needed and wanted. To fill that need he introduced *Advertising Age.* (With time *Ad Age* also included features, but these were highly specialized, and emphasized trends and marketing developments.)

When G. D. Crain died in 1973 at age 88 he left a prospering periodical business and a communications family empire that was to become even larger. *Advertising Age,* the company's flagship publication, grew from an initial free circulation of 7,000 to a worldwide paid circulation of over 80,000 and now has an annual subscription price of $40 (up from $1, the original price, to $10 in 1970). *Ad Age* today is "The International Newspaper of Marketing," and is published in two sections, the second covering a different subject or field of interest each week. *Printers Ink,* meanwhile, following change of ownership and title (*Marketing Communication*), ceased publication altogether in 1972.

In addition to *Advertising Age,* Crain Communications now publishes 15 other periodicals, including two area tabloid newspapers. It also has a book division, runs seminars, and is involved in other activities.

Moreover, it is still family owned and operated. Crain's widow, Gertrude Crain, who joined the company as assistant treasurer in 1941, is chairman of the board. The Crains' older son, Rance, is president and editor in chief, and the younger son, Keith, is vice chairman. Though not a relative, Sid Bernstein, chairman of the executive committee, who joined *Ad Age* in 1932 and was its editor, has long been a part of the Crain publishing family. He is credited with contributing to the success of *Ad Age* and of other company endeavors. He continues his editorial involvement with *Ad Age* in a number of ways, particularly in writing the weekly column, "con-Sid-erations."

Entrepreneurial Success Stories

Specialized business periodical publishing continues to be a growing and vital field. Each year an increasingly larger number of magazines are started, usually by editors or sales executives of existing periodicals who have fresh ideas. While not all of these magazines survive, many thrive. In the past decade, a number of noteworthy success stories have been recorded, all by small, independent publishers with an entrepreneurial flair. The remainder of this chapter describes several of these successes, with special attention given to *Computerworld* magazine.

FOLIO: THE MAGAZINE FOR MAGAZINE MANAGEMENT

In 1972 Joseph Hanson decided that no periodical existed for the managers of magazine publishers. So he started *Folio* that very year and is now both owner and publisher. But he had a difficult time selling advertising. His most likely prospects were paper manufacturers and printers. Paper firms, however, were involved in packaging and a variety of consumer-oriented products and thus advertised in consumer periodicals and packaging magazines. They did not need to advertise to publishers, they explained, because their production had been accounted for and presold (mostly to large consumer publishers and major distributors). As for advertising by printers, it was largely unheard of. While Hanson and his staff were able to generate some advertising from both categories (although mostly from printers), it was not enough to make *Folio* profitable. Nevertheless, Hanson was determined to stay in business. He decided on two steps to generate profits: First, to convert *Folio* to a totally paid periodical, starting with a then high subscription price of $18 per year (since increased to $42); and second, to develop an annual trade show for magazine publishers with concurrently run seminars on various magazine publishing operations.

Both steps turned out to be successful, with the resulting revenue more than enough to make *Folio* a viable, profitable business. In a short time, paid circulation reached 8,000 (it is now over 10,000). The Annual Publishing Conference and Exposition (for both magazine and book publishers) has become larger and more important each year, attracting 10,000 attendees in 1980. The success of the trade show has also insured the viability of the magazine, which now carries sufficient advertising to make it profitable on its own. Its October 1982 issue (containing the *Folio 400*/1982) was 646 pages and loaded with advertising.

INDUSTRY MEDIA, INC.

Charles Cleworth has displayed a special independent entrepreneurial spirit. One of two sons of C. William Cleworth, who built the successful Cleworth Publishing Company of Cos Cob, Connecticut, he decided to go on his own shortly after his father retired, having sold the company's most successful periodical, *Plastics World*, to Cahners Publishing Company. His brother, William, remained president of the family business, which now publishes two specialized electrical magazines. Charles moved to Denver and launched several highly specialized periodicals dealing with segments of the industry that had not been covered. His firm, Industry Media, Inc., now publishes *Plastics Compounding, Plastics Design Forum, Plastics Machinery & Equipment*, and *Plastics Machinery & Equipment Sourcebook for Extruders*.

Charles Cleworth is an innovator in other aspects of publishing. While more and more business periodical publishers are incorporating their own typesetting operations, Charles has gone further. Early in 1980, Industry Media installed a computer that is being utilized as "the front end" to operate its previously installed, high-speed, digitized phototypesetting equipment. Computer terminals have been set up at editors' desks, with similar terminals in the company's various departments, such as circulation and accounting. Thus, this fairly small publishing operation is among the most automated. In addition, Cleworth runs a number of regional plastics trade shows and seminars.

DELTA COMMUNICATIONS, INC.

Before its merger with IPC, Penton Publishing Company had acquired *Packaging Digest*, a new monthly tabloid product book. But after several years, the magazine still failed to meet budgetary requirements. William D'Alexander, who was publisher, and two colleagues on the publication then acquired the magazine in 1973 and set out on their own, forming Delta Communications, Inc., based in Chicago. They succeeded magnificently. Within a few years, *Packaging Digest* became the number one periodical covering the horizontal functions of the packaging field. During this time, *Modern Packaging* (the pioneer publication launched by Charles Breskin that was sold first to McGraw-Hill and then to Morgan-Grampian, the British-owned American subsidiary) went out of business and sold its title and other assets to Cahners' *Package Engineering*. Today, Delta Communications is expanding further, and has used earnings from *Packaging Digest* to acquire a magazine (*Furniture Design and Manufacturing*). In July of 1983 Delta acquired a packaging converting magazine.

D'Alexander and his associates have demonstrated what single-minded entrepreneurs can do with a publication considered a failure by a large publishing operation. By improving the editorial product and through aggressive advertising sales, they increased circulation and advertising revenue, albeit not without risk on their part.

COMPUTERWORLD AND OTHER COMPUTER MAGAZINES

One of the most successful, if not *the* most successful, publishers of specialized business magazines of the past decade did not begin his career with a journalism degree. Patrick J. McGovern, publisher of *Computerworld* and an international group of other computer-related specialized periodicals, launched his career in 1959 following graduation from the Massachusetts Institute of Technology with a bachelor of science degree in computer engineering and applications. His first job was as an associate editor of *Computers and Automation* magazine, a leading monthly at that time. By 1964 he had started International Data Corporation (IDC), a marketing research and consulting firm specializing in the computer field. In 1967 he launched *Computerworld*, a magazine that has enjoyed explosive popularity.

Here is the why and how of *Computerworld*: While working at *Computers and Automation* and as head of IDC, McGovern noticed that whereas there were seven magazines in the computer field, most doing exceptionally well, they were all monthlies and almost all dealt with the "how to" of the business. McGovern was convinced that the fast-growing, and continually changing field needed a weekly, news-oriented periodical. *Computerworld* was the answer. The success of the weekly tabloid exceeded even McGovern's expectations, and the publication soon outdistanced its competitors.

The three elements that made *Computerworld* a success, according to McGovern, were "research, research, and research." Prior to launching the magazine, McGovern and his associates at IDC spent three years and invested over $1 million in developing a comprehensive census of computer installations in the United States. This data base formed a uniquely accurate and comprehensive circulation base for *Computerworld*. Through numerous industry-sponsored studies, McGovern and his staff identified the products, the application of such products, and the technology-information needs of computer users and industry executives, information that served as the basis for *Computerworld*'s editorial focus. In addition, the periodical had available (through IDC research) extensive information on the market objectives, sales volumes, and business goals and objectives of the principal advertising prospects for *Computerworld*.

Since McGovern had only limited experience in the production and distribution of a magazine, it took several years of trial and error to properly shape these operations. Instead of going the way of controlled, or free, distribution, as had the other established computer magazines, McGovern decided to launch

Computerworld on a paid subscription basis. For one thing, McGovern reasoned, the new periodical needed the subscription revenue to survive its start-up period (one could not know how fast or how extensively advertisers would begin placing advertising). Besides, McGovern did not want to be under pressure to sell advertising at an early stage. It was the right approach. The magazine's fast growth to 100,000 paid subscriptions testifies to a superior editorial product that is finely tuned, through readership research, to the needs of its audience, and to a comprehensive direct-mail program to grab the attention of persons and firms entering the computer field.

Computerworld, as part of a publishing company now called CW Communications, Inc., with over $40 million in annual billing, is by far the world's largest and most successful publication on computers, and CW Communications is the largest publisher in the computer field worldwide. *Computerworld* has also given birth to a family of computer-related publications around the world. The company now publishes *Computer Business News*, a weekly in the United States, as well as *InfoWorld*, a biweekly for the microcomputer and personal computer field. In England, the company publishes a weekly called *Computerworld/UK*, as well as a monthly magazine titled *Computer Management*. In Japan, it publishes the weekly *Shukan Dempa Computer*; in Australia, the weekly *Australian Computerworld*; in Brazil, the biweekly *Data News*; and, more recently, *China Computerworld*, in the People's Republic of China.

According to McGovern, the company's growth has been largely through international expansion. He believes that it can maintain its 35 percent annual corporate growth rate without expanding much beyond the computer and data processing fields in the decade ahead. Beyond that? There appears no limit to McGovern's publishing creativity.

McGovern's unprecedented success underscores the importance of several basic ingredients for launching a specialized business periodical. Two of these basic ingredients are familiarity with and special knowledge of the industry to be covered by the magazine, and editorial and publishing experience. Of the two, knowledge and identification with an industry appears more crucial and often entails special education, training, and several years' involvement with the industry. Learning to edit and publish a magazine can be accomplished in a shorter time. Also required is comprehensive research to determine the specific audience, market, and editorial and advertising approaches to be adopted. In addition, the development of an effective circulation list and an analysis of whether to go "controlled" or "paid" are necessary. While an intelligently planned budget and adequate start-up financing are also necessary, the elements on which McGovern based his *Computerworld* triumph are more important in the long run.

Structure and Function of the Business Press

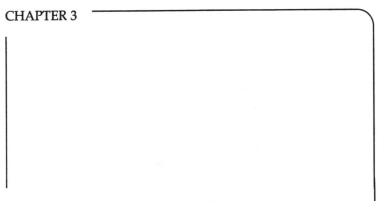

CHAPTER 3

The Business Journalist

What preparation is required for a career in business journalism? A journalism degree is definitely an asset in obtaining a beginner's position, whether on a big city daily, in broadcasting, on a general news magazine, or in the specialized business press. But a journalism degree is not absolutely necessary. A college degree with a major in English and a good overall record will often be sufficient. Courses in economics, accounting, general law, and business administration can also be helpful. (See Chapter 9 for further discussion.)

What is most essential for the business journalist is a special interest in the business world. For the specialized periodical journalist, knowledge of the workings of a certain industry (or group of industries) eventually becomes essential. An editor of a nutrition magazine, for example, will be required to learn as much as possible about the entire food business and its various subdivisions. An acquaintance with key executives will also become valuable. Similarly, the editor of an electronics magazine is more likely to perform well if he or she has had some education or training in electronic engineering. A professional business journalist may be described as one who understands and can "talk" the language of the business. In addition to keeping track of important developments in the field, a professional journalist should eventually become perceptive enough to sense new trends in the industry. Such expertise is typically obtained through on-the-job experience.

Basic Abilities of a Business Journalist

What are some basic abilities of a competent editor in business journalism? In general, they are the skills required of any journalist and include:

1. The ability to write well. Added to this is the ability to edit well—to take something already written and, if necessary, to transform it into concise, readable prose that fits the special tone of a publication.
2. The ability to sense what's newsworthy—to seek out the core of a story (i.e., to have a reporter's "nose"). Asking the right questions and getting to the heart of the matter—or "finding the lead"—is a basic skill for a successful journalist.
3. The ability to listen carefully and with an open mind.
4. The skill to absorb material, which requires the ability to take notes both physically and mentally. (Use of a mechanical transcriber can be helpful, but it can sometimes prove distracting.)
5. The ability to take, and follow through on, directions.
6. Good typing skill, preferably "touch" typing, with at least modest speed.

Special Abilities of a Business Journalist

Because the business journalist is a specialized professional, he or she needs special skills or knowledge. Following are areas that are particularly important:

1. A knowledge of the business world, with special emphasis on the relevant industry or profession. While acquiring this knowledge is a long-term process, some understanding of the particular industry (or profession) is needed at the outset.
2. An appreciation of the business community—what it is, how it works, its goals, its philosophy, and its function in society.
3. Ability to communicate with the business community. While

every good journalist must be a good communicator, business journalists have a special need to maintain direct and perhaps more frequent contact with the people and industries they serve. The more a journalist learns about a particular business—often through conversations with industry spokespersons—the greater is his or her understanding of new products, developments, and trends. Journalists often perceive new developments before industry executives do. In addition, they can be catalysts in the development of new products and marketing approaches. (Not infrequently, the journalist may be called upon to present talks to industry groups or to serve on industry committees.)

The following scenario demonstrates the unique blend of talent and information that characterizes a successful journalist on a specialized business magazine.

Imagine that the editor of a packaging magazine is to interview the packaging executive of a large, highly competitive food manufacturing and marketing company. The purpose of the interview is to discuss the introduction of a new line of products, with emphasis on the packaging to be used. The product is a frozen pudding, in a variety of flavors, which will compete directly with existing and widely marketed frozen desserts from a number of established ice cream manufacturers.

In order to conduct a successful interview, the business editor must be knowledgeable about the frozen desserts with which the new product line will compete, their packaging, and the special functions served by their packaging materials. He or she must also understand the motivation behind the new line of products. In posing questions, the editor must be prepared to talk knowledgeably about the new packaging materials and their function, as well as about design, graphics, and color. Other topics that may be discussed include how the packages will help the marketing approach, their contribution to the "shelf life" of the product, and other factors that will allow the products to take a planned share of the market.

Throughout the interview, the editor must also be able to put the executive at ease so that he or she will be willing to answer all key questions—and perhaps tell the editor a bit more. The basis is thus laid for a first-rate article about the new products, as well as for a profile of the executive.

Following the interview, the editor will meet with the company's marketing chief and, finally, with the executive responsible for the design of the new product line. In each case, the editor should be able to "speak the language" of the person being interviewed.

The editor must then return to the office and write the story— possibly a cover feature of interest to an important segment of the periodical's readership.

It should be apparent that editors of specialized business magazines are exceptional in being both specialists and generalists—specialists in that they are fully informed about one or a group of industries, and generalists in that they are able to use their talents of interviewing, researching, and writing in almost any area covered by a specialized magazine.

Although there are specialists in the consumer press, too— such as the drama critic or the medical writer—by and large, a journalist for the consumer press, and particularly a newspaper reporter or editor, is a generalist who can be assigned to cover any number of different kinds of stories.

Specific Functions of the Specialized Business Journalist

The specific functions of the specialized business journalist vary with the publication and the industry served. Typically, these duties include: researching new products and developments; scanning news releases; reviewing competing magazines; editing and rewriting; interviewing business executives (in person and by telephone); creating and writing original feature articles (including plant stories); developing (or being assigned to write) columns of specific reader interest; attending and covering conventions, trade shows, seminars, and various other meetings; and reporting on new products and technological developments.

An editor in training on a specialized business periodical has an exceptional opportunity to learn almost all aspects of magazine production, including: writing and editing copy; type marking; writing heads, subheads, and captions; taking and cropping photographs; dummying copy; and working with the production and art departments on the graphics and layout of the periodical—from suggesting specific illustrations to page design, positioning of advertising, use of color, and imposition of the publication. (Knowledge of graphics is often acquired on the job.)

The extent of the editor's involvement in these areas will depend on the type and size of the publishing company. The larger the company, the more departmentalized is the work. An editor working for a smaller company, on the other hand, may be required to perform every function necessary to plan and produce a periodical. Though the trend has been toward medium-size and large multi-periodical publishing operations, which normally have separate production and art departments, knowledge by an editor of the entire production process can enhance a publication and ensure smoother communications between the editorial and art/production departments.

Career Outlook

The future in business periodicals is brighter than ever. As has been pointed out, every year a number of new business magazines are launched, some of which cover new industries while others cover new functions of existing industries. New periodicals always spell employment opportunities for editors as well as for personnel in various allied fields such as circulation, advertising space selling, and management.

It should be noted that job-hopping in the specialized business press is much less frequent than in other media. Beginners change positions more often than others; once a business journalist finds a niche, chances are he or she will move up the ladder of that publication. Business periodical editors and publishers prefer to promote from within rather than hire outsiders for senior positions. This is because a business periodical journalist who has been with a publishing company several years possesses a wealth of information about a particular industry. The journalist develops an "investment" in a particular field, and, in turn, the publication develops an "investment" in the editor. When experienced editors do change jobs, it is often to a competing periodical, or to launch one of their own.

It is also important to remember that changes in the marketplace occur continually, providing new opportunities for expansion of existing magazines or the creation of new ones. Here, too, employment opportunities develop.

Area Business Publications

So-called area business publications constitute a comparatively new market of business journalism that has grown explosively since the late 1970s: by 1982 there were approximately 50 such publications, and new periodicals were appearing regularly. Those involved with publications of this kind have even formed their own trade association, the Association of Area Business Publications.

What exactly is an area business publication? Simply stated, it is a periodical that deals with the business news of a particular city, state, region, or marketing area. Such periodicals have typically been published as standard-size magazines or tabloid newspapers and issued weekly, biweekly, or monthly.

Local daily newspapers have, until recently, generally done a poor job of business reporting, while the national business magazines have traditionally concentrated on national and international news. Nor has the specialized business press been able to devote much space to local business developments. Area business periodicals are now filling this void, and some are experiencing marked success. The largest area periodical is *California Business*, with 55,000 paid and 15,000 controlled circulation. *Chicago Business* has a circulation of 40,000; and *Texas Business, Florida Trend*, and *New England Business* each have a circulation of 35,000. The mushrooming of these publications is in direct response to two separate marketing opportunites: (1) A growing number of readers, who, for efficiency's sake, are choosing to read one national business publication and one local publication and (2) more selective advertisers, who are seeking a more efficient means of matching media with target markets, both geographically and demographically.

The growth of these periodicals also results from dramatic changes in the national business community. Not many years ago, the brains, power, and action of the national business scene were concentrated in a few major business, financial, and industrial centers—for example, New York and Chicago. In the past two decades, however, a growing number of regional centers have developed. For example, business people no longer have to go to New York, Chicago, or San Francisco for capital investment loans or to negotiate any number of other business transactions. Local banks now provide many such services. Accordingly, business people need to be informed as to the character of their local business communities to a greater degree than in the past. Area business periodicals serve this function.

Some area business periodicals are now part of group publishing operations, a trend sure to continue. Cordovan Publishing Company, for example, launched the *Houston Business Journal*, a weekly tabloid, in 1970. In 1978, Cordovan followed with a similar publication in Atlanta. Now the company has business tabloids in Seattle, San Francisco, Los Angeles, San Diego, Miami, and Phoenix. Cordovan is owned by Scripps-Howard Newspapers. Other daily newspaper chains may well get into the field of area periodicals, and will probably favor the weekly tabloid style.

In a few instances, the specialized business press has expanded into area business periodicals, the best example being Crain Communications, Inc., in Chicago. In late 1978, Crain introduced *Chicago Business*, a weekly newspaper. It was an immediate success, and now has the second largest circulation in the area business publication field. Crain is planning other area business periodicals.

Area business publications offer new employment opportunities not only for business journalists but for all types of publishing personnel. Such publications may well serve as a training ground for business journalists hoping to enter the national business media.

The growth and success of area business publications also serves to demonstrate the energy and vitality of the business journalism field, and may be indicative of the potential of other as yet undiscovered directions in business journalism.

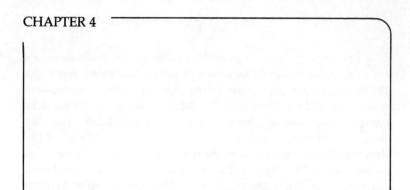

CHAPTER 4

Business News for the Consumer

In this century, business news (and economics in general) has been given some attention in the consumer press, especially the daily newspaper; but it was not until the mid-1970s that the consumer press really "discovered" the appeal of business news for the general public and the revenue potential from advertising.

The genesis of this "awakening" may be found in the growth of both general business periodicals and the specialized business press, and the huge success of *The Wall Street Journal*. The consumer press quickly realized that it had to position itself to obtain a share of this readership and advertising potential—not by competing directly with the specialized business press, since readership and advertising in this area are highly specialized, but by demonstrating to business-oriented readers that the consumer press could also provide valuable information.

The Daily Press Gets Down to Business

In order to compete with *The Wall Street Journal* and with general business periodicals such as *Business Week, Forbes, Industry Week, Fortune, Barron's,* and *Dun's Review* (now *Dun's Business Month*), the larger daily newspapers, led by *The New York Times*, formulated a program for expanded business news coverage.

THE NEW YORK TIMES

The New York Times, which had long published more business news than any other daily newspaper, took a bold step in May 1978 by introducing a separate section called "Business Day" five days a week. Its "Saturday Business Day" forms part of "Metropolitan Report." *The Sunday New York Times* has had a business section for many years, but in 1981 the section was redesigned and the name changed to "Business."

"Business Day" is normally 20 pages long. Its compelling front page includes a left-hand side bar (comprising two of the page's six columns) called "Business Digest," consisting of section headlines and brief summaries of each section. Section titles may include, for example, International, Companies, Markets, The Economy, and Today's Columns. Stories selected for coverage are timely and, in general, of national or international importance.

The *Times* has close to 70 staff members in New York serving "Business Day," about 35 of whom are reporters, all working under the direction of Business Editor John M. Lee. In addition, it has a "backfield" of about eight editors who assign, organize, and supervise the daily business report, plus a copy desk of a dozen or so employees. The business news department also has its own art, graphics, and design staff of four.

Outside the New York headquarters, the *Times* business news department employs six economic specialists on the Washington, D.C. staff, who write largely on "Business Day," as well as a group of *Times* correspondents in Detroit, Chicago, Los Angeles, and cities around the world. (The *Times* also has access to all *Times*' correspondents as well as a large stringer network.)

The *Sunday Times* "Business" section has a separate staff of editors, although it uses the same pool of reporters as "Business Day."

What kind of background does the *Times* require of its business news staff? While there are no special requirements, most are college graduates, and graduate degrees in law, business, economics, engineering, and journalism are common. Almost all of the writers came to the *Times* with experience as editors on other publications. The median age is about 32.

Reader reaction to the *Times'* expanded business coverage and revised format has been overwhelmingly favorable. The complete financial tables and expanded coverage of technology and such fields as management, accounting, and law have drawn especially positive comment. In addition, the magazine-like organization of *Business Day* (with predictably placed departments) and its strong graphics have been well received.

The Times' example was soon followed by other major newspapers across the country, some of which had been providing business and financial news for many years. The American Newspaper Publishers Association had a membership of 1,405 companies (as of late 1981) which included 1,745 daily, 735 Sunday, and 7,602 weekly newspapers. Today, many, but far from most, daily newspapers have special business sections (published once or several times weekly), and most provide at least some business and financial news, largely of a local nature. Only the larger dailies publish full New York and American stock exchange trading results tables.

While the quality and amount of coverage of *The New York Times'* "Business Day" and "Sunday's Business" are difficult to equal, a few other newspapers come close, including *The Boston Globe* (discussed later), *The Washington Post, The Chicago Tribune* (also discussed later), *The Kansas City Star, The Philadelphia Inquirer,* and *The San Francisco Chronicle.*

KNIGHT-RIDDER NEWSPAPERS, INC.

Among newspaper chains (and the number of independently owned daily newspapers is dwindling fast), the Knight-Ridder Newspapers, Inc., a combination of the Knight and Ridder chains, provides business news in all of its daily newspapers; but only the larger of its newspapers have regular sections. Among these are *The Miami Herald*, which has a daily "Business News" section and a much larger "Business Monday" in tabloid format; *The San Jose Mercury News*, with a section called "Business," both weekdays and on Sunday; *The Detroit Free Press*, with a daily and Sunday section called "Business"; and *The Philadelphia Inquirer* (mentioned earlier—an average-quality newspaper prior to its acquisition by Knight, but today the city's leading daily. *The Inquirer's* increased business coverage contributed to its new status).

NEWHOUSE NEWSPAPERS

Newhouse Newspapers, which publishes 25 dailies across the country, provides coverage of business and financial news in all of its papers, but only a few have special daily (or less frequent) business/financial sections. Nevertheless, the chain is seeing a trend toward special business sections. Beginning in the first quarter of 1981, ten of its newspapers started annual business and financial reviews, some of substantial size. Newhouse also owns the Syracuse, New York, newspapers and the Booth newspaper chain, and several papers in both chains are slated to have annual reviews, most to be published on Sunday.

Among the leading Newhouse newspapers in quality of business coverage are *The Birmingham News, The Cleveland Plain Dealer, The Mississippi Press-Register, The St. Louis Post/Globe,* and *The Springfield Republican.*

THE BOSTON GLOBE

As mentioned earlier, *The Boston Globe* is doing an excellent job of covering business news. In April 1980, to supplement its daily business section, it added a unique Tuesday "Business Extra" consisting of 16 to 20 pages. The emphasis is on local coverage, although the section does contain substantial national and some international business news. The section is almost totally staff-written except for a few columnists. According to Gordon McKibben, business editor, the Boston business community, which had long felt "short-changed" in relation to other urban business centers, welcomed the attention provided by the new Tuesday section. The section has also succeeded with the general reader. Mr. McKibben stated:

> "I think it has succeeded with general readers in the sense that we look for humor, for 'drama,' for pain and peril, and all other aspects

of good stories that are just as much a part of business journalism as 'general.' We have put a lot of stress on profiles. We try to provide a good bit of consumer-oriented information, but we do not write 'down' and we do assume a sense of intelligence and curiosity on the part of our readers. We interpret 'business' as a very broad subject area."

The Globe's special business editorial staff consists of 20 reporters, editors, copy desk workers, and secretaries. In addition, The Globe employs a technology/computer writer with prior experience on a specialized business periodical and an economics writer with strong ties to academia and previous experience writing for Forbes. The remaining business news reporters and editors have general newspaper backgrounds, some with special "beats" within business, such as Wall Street, banking/finance, labor and transportation, and investments. Interestingly, several of the younger staff members had earlier worked primarily in business journalism for other daily newspapers and were thus committed to business writing. In the future, newspapers wishing to upgrade their business news coverage may increasingly tap such talent. Then, too, business writers of daily newspapers often become editors of specialized business magazines; others go to major general business magazines or become business editors on the weekly news magazines; still others join the business news staffs of broadcasting companies.

GANNETT, INC.

The Gannett Company, Inc., with headquarters in Rochester, New York, is one of the largest newspaper chains in the United States, and the coverage of business news in its papers has been receiving increasing emphasis. Almost all of its so-called middle-size and larger newspapers (with circulations of 40,000 and up) now have business news departments and/or regular business news pages, on a weekly, twice weekly, or daily basis. In recent years, many of Gannett's papers have also expanded the space devoted to business news. For example, both of Gannett's Rochester, New York, newspapers have doubled the size of their daily business news "hold"—from two to four pages—and have nearly doubled the size of their staffs. Many of the chain's smaller newspapers have also recently added new pages or columns of local business news.

As a form of "inservice training," Gannett conducts seminars to help its business editors and reporters improve their knowledge of economics as well as their writing skills. Many of the chain's business journalists have also attended special fellowship programs in economics at various U.S. colleges.

While Gannett has no special educational requirements for business journalists (having frequently transferred them from general news reporting), it has followed a policy of encouraging them to enter university-level economics programs.

Here are examples of increases in Gannett business news staffs among its medium-size newspapers. In 1976, for example, the staff of the Rochester, New York, *Democrat & Chronicle* business department numbered four. By 1982 the department had a staff of seven, with plans for additional positions. At the *Rochester Times-Union*, the staff was increased from four to eight. And at the Oakland *Tribune/Eastbay Today*, a newspaper that has enjoyed remarkable growth in the San Francisco Bay area, the business news staff was increased from four to seven and the business news hold moved from three to five pages daily.

Among Gannett's smaller newspapers which have increased business news coverage are *The Lafayette* (Indiana) *Journal and Courier* and *The Battle Creek* (Michigan) *Enquirer-News*. Both have increased their business news hold by 50 percent and now cover business news daily as do many other Gannett newspapers.

In mid-1982, following considerable research, Gannett launched *USA Today*, a national newspaper, with a present circulation of 1,000,000.

THE CHICAGO TRIBUNE

The Chicago Tribune, one of the country's major newspapers, has been expanding its business coverage, too. In September 1976 *The Tribune* added a full page of business news to its Monday business section. The plan was eventually to expand to sizable daily business sections, each with a different emphasis. The extra Monday page was labeled the "Monday A.M. Business Report" and was designed to cover weekend national and foreign news. It included a calendar of events and short articles on important business news events upcoming during the week, the idea being to bring business executives up to date as they went to work Monday morning.

Wednesday's business page, the next to expand, focused on business news of Chicago and the Midwest. In April 1978, this page was greatly expanded to form a separate section called the Midwest Business Report. Again, the emphasis was on Chicago and the Midwest, with special attention given to local and national securities markets, small business, labor, and company trends.

In November 1978, the Sunday business section was enlarged to a separate, free-standing section providing in-depth examinations of the week's business happenings, as well as other vital business stories.

Two years later, in March 1980, the Tuesday business section was also expanded, and now focuses on money management both for business persons and consumers.

In October 1981, *The Tribune* started publishing an "International Business Section" on Thursday, as well as an expanded Friday business section, devoted to general business news. Both have additional space and both are now separate sections.

In the meantime, the Monday section has been revamped to emphasize "working," a term *The Tribune* uses to describe the entire job environment. The stories deal with a variety of subjects, from management to office design, including the impact on the worker.

In the course of this expansion, *The Tribune's* staff has grown from 8 to 28 business journalists, largely business news reporters hired from *The Wall Street Journal, Newsweek, Business Week,* United Press Internationl, and Reuters, Ltd.

Reader reaction has been positive. In letters and telephone calls to the paper, readers say they want more business news— news that can help them to keep abreast of current business events or to cope better with inflation, business problems, and their jobs.

SCRIPPS-HOWARD NEWSPAPERS

Of the 16 Scripps-Howard Newspaper chains, five provide special business sections or devote considerable space daily to business news (most of the others also regularly publish some business and financial news). The five are: *The Pittsburgh Press, The
Commercial Appeal* (Memphis), *The Rocky Mountain News* (Denver),
The Cincinnati Post, and the *San Juan Star* (Puerto Rico). Each has
a business editor and a business staff. *The Rocky Mountain News*
has the largest business staff of the chain.

The General Business Magazine

As has been stated, the growth and success of general business
magazines in the United States has been a special phenomenon
in business journalism, and is largely the result of greater interest
in the business world by a more sophisticated general public and
by business management. The trend has been strengthened by
the increasing interest of women in finances and by the disrup-
tion caused in the world economy by inflation. The "big five"
general business magazines are *Business Week, Forbes*, Barron's
Industry Week, Fortune, and *Dun's Business Month* (the former *Dun's
Review*). Short portraits of each of these periodicals were contained in Chapter 1; the following descriptions focus on the editorial objectives and structure of each.

BUSINESS WEEK

Business Week, the preeminent periodical of McGraw-Hill Publications Company (the second most profitable division of McGraw-
Hill, Inc.), passed the $1 billion revenue mark in 1980. *Business
Week* has the largest circulation (777,000) of the top five general
business magazines, the biggest share of advertising (over $130
million), and a record of continued growth. Editor-in-Chief Lewis
H. Young, a veteran of 13 years with the magazine, and his staff

edit a magazine that covers every major (and some minor) facets of the business world. *Business Week's* articles are generally well-researched, timely, and despite specialized subject matter, are written to appeal to a broad segment of the business community. In addition to the cover story and other basic features, each issue highlights the week's news under such regular headlines as The Economy, Money & Credit, Capitol Hill, Housing, Acquisitions, Aviation, Regulators, World Trade, and Entertainment. Each issue also includes two newsletters, "Business Outlook" and "Personal Business," and a full page "Business Week Index" that includes production levels, prices, and other indicators. Regular departments include Accounting, Books (reviews), Corporate Strategies, Economic Diary, Energy, International Business, Media & Advertising, Labor and Management, and others.

Business Week is the only business weekly published in the United States: *Forbes, Industry Week*, and *Fortune* are biweeklies, and *Dun's Business Month* is a monthly.

FORBES

In my opinion, the most successful and exciting of the biweeklies is *Forbes*. Like *Business Week*, it covers the entire gamut of business. Unlike the other business oriented periodicals, however, *Forbes* largely expresses the personality of its president and editor-in-chief, Malcolm S. Forbes, Jr., whose father, B. C. Forbes, founded the magazine in 1917. Forbes' biweekly, several-page column, "Fact and Comment," which deals with almost anything (including reviews of New York restaurants), reflects his zest for life, his intelligence, and his humor, and generally concludes with an appropriately pithy comment such as, "Why is it so many want to be what they're not, while what they are is what others want to be?"

Forbes also differs from the other general business periodicals in that it features seven financial columnists, most of whom offer stock and other financial advice and comment. (*Forbes* does not compete with *Barron's National Business and Financial Weekly*, the financial tabloid published by Dow Jones & Company, Inc., which is a financial journal exclusively.)

INDUSTRY WEEK

Industry Week, the biweekly published by Penton/IPC, a division of the Pittway Corporation, has matured substantially since it was converted from *Steel* in 1969. It now enjoys a special niche in the business community. It differs from the other general business magazines in that it is basically for middle management, although it covers all aspects of business, primarily in the form of features rather than news reports (for example, it does not regularly carry financial reports).

Unlike *Business Week* and *Forbes, Industry Week* has a controlled circulation. Its circulation started at 130,000 and in the course of six phases of circulation development was increased by 1982 to a circulation of over 300,000. Although the magazine's emphasis is on middle management, its readers now include both top and middle management in a long list of varied industries, as well as utilities, finance, insurance, and business services.

The editorial objective of *Industry Week* is to provide multiple solutions to problems facing the executive. It thus suggests ways to improve personal productivity, increase corporate profitability, and help others to maximize the motivations and rewards of work. While the magazine reports on and interprets events affecting industry, particular attention is devoted to innovations in managerial techniques. Most of its editorial content is staff-written, with occasional articles by noted authorities in the business community and academia.

Industry Week's advertising revenue in 1982 passed $16 million compared with $3,743,000 in 1970, its first full year of operation.

FORTUNE

Fortune, the beautifully illustrated Time, Inc., business magazine founded in February 1930, was converted from a monthly to a biweekly in January 1978, and the overall size was changed from an oversized format to 9 1/2 by 10 3/4 inches. Except for shorter features, however, it is basically the same. While its "In the News" department interprets selected news developments of the biweekly period, with emphasis on the people (usually top management) who make the news, the magazine does not attempt comprehensive coverage of business news. Its hallmarks are its features, diverse in subject matter, well researched, and well written. (Examples of departments and headline articles that appeared in the September 21, 1981, issue are: *Government*: "Reagan's First 200 Days"; *Retailing*: "K Mart's Plan to Be Born Again, Again"; *Finance*: "The Trade in Tax Breaks Takes Off"; *Picture Portfolio*: "Tailors for the Tutored Eye"; and *Securities*: "The Mighty Mouse of Block Trading." Among the issue's departments were: Fortune Forecast, Keeping Up, Personal Investing, and Books and Ideas. It is designed for top management, and the up-and-coming young executive.

Fortune celebrated its fiftieth anniversary with its February 11, 1980, issue. In 50 years it has grown considerably. In 1930, *Fortune* published 779 pages of advertising, remarkable for the first year of a magazine launched during the depression. Its 1981 advertising volume exceeded 2,500 pages and its circulation had grown from 30,000 in 1930 to 670,000.

Dun's Review (now *Dun's Business Month*), the long-time Dun & Bradstreet Corporation monthly, had for years lacked specific editorial definition. In September 1981, following careful study of the needs of its audience of business executives, the magazine was redesigned and its name changed to *Dun's Business Month*. The transformation was total, including not only graphics but editorial content. Its now well-defined editorial approach, developed by Editor Clem Morgello and Publisher Robert A. Potts, aims (in Potts' words) "to provide information-overdosed executives with a monthly overview." A special feature of the new approach is an analysis of "the significant developments of the past month" under the department "The Business Month."

The new *Dun's Business Month* is designed to be read selectively. Stated Morgello in the first issue:

> "We are confident you will come across many items that are not new. . . . Skip them. We are confident you will come across many other items that are new. Other executives may read the items you skip, and skip the items you read."

In order to make selective reading easy, virtually the entire periodical has been departmentalized under titles such as Washington, Economy, Companies, Money and Markets, Labor, Industries, Marketing, Communications, Technology, and Cities and States, among others.

The magazine now also contains a number of well-planned features—for example, "A New Era for Bell—and Everyone Else" and "Flexible Benefits Are Spreading Fast"—and other short, typically one-page features.

Will the new *Dun's Business Month* succeed? It appears to be on the right track.

Time and *Newsweek* Get into the Act

More and more general consumer magazines are now dealing with aspects of the business world. Of the more than 700 general magazines representing the membership of the Magazine Publishers Association, Inc., almost half now have at least occasional articles on business. And many more are expected to follow this trend in the years ahead. While some features are staff written, most are assigned to outside contributors.

Most business features in general consumer magazines deal with personalities in the business world. For example, the article, "What Makes Janet Tanner Tick?" in the August 1981 issue of *Life*, tells the reader what it means to be a successful woman executive in the 1980s and how Tanner got there, and gives a picture of some of the workings of a large business enterprise.

Even *Reader's Digest*, the "digest-size" monthly for the general public, with a worldwide circulation of 31 million (1981), covers some phases of the business world in most of its issues. For example, the August 1981 issue carried an article entitled, "How Japan Does It—Can We Do It Too?" (reprinted from *Time*, March 30, 1981) that dealt with the competition being given American industry by Japanese-made products.

Of the consumer magazines, *Newsweek* and *Time* have made the most ambitious effort (but with only limited success) to publish news and features relating to business. Their major objective has been to obtain a slice of business-oriented advertising from general business magazines and the specialized business press. Considerable promotional efforts and direct selling are being used to that end.

Both *Time* and *Newsweek* have weekly sections on business; *Newsweek* calls its section simply "Business," while that in *Time* is called "Economy & Business." Both sections contain short features on people, products, and developments.

Neither magazine has been very successful in capturing a meaningful segment of business advertising, however, although each carries some corporate-oriented advertising.

The Broadcast Media

Thus far, radio and television have not taken significant steps in the direction of business coverage, although efforts are being made. Each of the major networks (ABC, CBS, and NBC) now employs business news editors, the best known being Ray Brady of CBS.

The Public Broadcasting Service (PBS) presently offers three popular business-related television programs for consumers: "Inside Business Today," "The Nightly Business Report," and "Wall Street Week."

"Inside Business Today," which airs on Saturdays, treats a different aspect of business every week, focusing on subjects such as starting a retail store, marketing to minorities, and so forth. "Inside Business Today" reaches close to 45,000 households. In contrast, "The Nightly Business Report," which appears every weekday evening, reaches close to half a million households.

"The Nightly Business Report" not only reviews stock market closings but also features commentary on business trends and in-depth consideration of particular industries. One program on the state of the computer industry, for example, examined the Knight-Ridder videotext system being introduced in Florida; discussed the donation of computer equipment to San Diego County schools by various manufacturers; and featured an interview with the president of the Tandy Corporation on anticipated future developments in the industry.

One of the most popular shows on PBS television is "Wall Street Week," hosted by Louis Rukeyser. "Must" watching for many investors each Friday night, the show is viewed by close to two million people. In addition to covering weekly developments in the stock market and answering viewers' questions on investing, the show features a different guest-expert each week, who might be an economist or a presidential advisor or a noted securities analyst.

Starting March 1, 1983, a new program called "Business Times" began broadcasting under the sponsorship of ESPN (Entertainment and Sport Programming Network), a two-hour (6 to 8 A.M. in the East and 5 to 7 A.M. in the Midwest) program dealing with business and financial news developments. A special editorial staff has been appointed to deal with this program. Included are writers and editors who were former staff members on *Business Week, Newsweek,* and *The Economist.* Aiding the "Business Times" editorial staff will be the *Financial Times of London.*

Other such business programs over the airways may follow, especially from cable network or local cable stations.

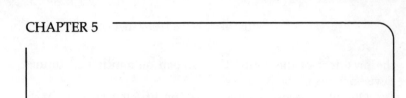

CHAPTER 5

Editing and Publishing a Specialized Business Periodical

This chapter deals with the editorial preparation and production of four representative specialized business periodicals: a monthly tabloid-style magazine, two standard-size monthly magazines, and a weekly tabloid.

The periodicals selected focus on different industries and vary in size of staff, size of average issue, circulation, and editorial approach. Each editor has his or her own special way of tackling the problem of "putting the magazine to bed" (i.e., getting it on the press). Nevertheless, the overall process is much the same.

Let us look first at a tabloid-style monthly. (For definitions of unfamiliar terms, readers are referred to the Glossary of Terms at the end of this book.)

Food & Drug Packaging

Food & Drug Packaging, a news- and feature-oriented tabloid printed on a good quality coated paper on a web press, has a controlled circulation in excess of 65,000. Originally launched as a biweekly, it is now published monthly. Four-color printing (both for advertising and editorial copy) is used extensively. As a biweekly the periodical averaged 46 pages per issue, while as a monthly it averages 64 pages per issue, with some issues running 100 pages or more.

Food & Drug Packaging is an award-winning periodical; in 1980 its editors received the Jesse Neal Award of the American Business Press (considered the Pulitzer Prize of the specialized business press).

Originally founded by Magazines For Industry, Inc., which merged with Harcourt Brace Jovanovich, Inc., in mid-1982, *Food & Drug Packaging* is now one of the 111 periodicals published by HBJ Publications, a division of Harcourt Brace Jovanovich.

Food & Drug Packaging has a full-time editorial staff of four, and a technical editor, who serves on retainer. The magazine also uses the part-time services of a Washington editorial group and free-lance correspondents in the United States and other countries.

Though there are two other monthly packaging magazines, one standard-size and the other a tabloid, *Food & Drug Packaging* alone specializes in the $400 billion (combined) food and drug and allied packaging industries, which together represent about 80 percent of the total packaging field. The magazine's contents consist of news, features, and departments, generally relating to the "how" and "why" of good packaging concepts and technology. The magazine features, in addition, a monthly profile of a packaging person in the news and interviews with leading executives. There is also a section devoted to new products—equipment, materials, and services.

Food & Drug Packaging has become a "spokesperson" on behalf of the industry, both in the marketplace and as a source for governmental agencies. The magazine's executive editor, Ben Miyares, served as president of the Packaging Institute, in addition to directing seminars and speaking before numerous groups. The magazine's technical editor has also contributed enormously to the periodical, not only by virtue of his expertise in the packaging field, but because of his participation in industry seminars and trade gatherings as well.

Following is an outline of the editorial and production procedures involved in producing a typical issue, as prepared by the editor and his staff.

. Functions of Editor
    A. Gathering information (sources):
        • Press releases

- Press conferences
- Visits to businesses
- Seminars
- Industry meetings
- Salespersons
- Advertisers
- Published sources
- Personal contacts

B. Editor evaluates each possible story and feature, asking:
  - Is this of interest to our readers?
  - Is it new?
  - Will it affect their businesses or careers?
  - Are they likely to know this already?
  - Is it within the scope of the publication?
  - Can we provide supplier credits, such as origin and specific source of information obtained, including names of industry suppliers?
  - Is it a packaging story?
  - Can we get it on an exclusive basis or can we provide unique information?

C. Editor assigns stories to reporters/editors according to:
  - Expertise
  - Interest
  - Availability
  - Geography

D. Editor sets deadlines and suggests length, treatment:
  - Feature article or news item?
  - Short or long?
  - Up front or in back of the book?

E. Editor discusses significance of stories with reporters/editors:
  - Is it part of a trend?
  - Is there an unusual aspect to the story?
  - What is the importance to the reader?

- What was the impact of similar stories on the readership?
- Is the story sufficiently different?

F. Editor discusses with editor/reporter the type of available contact(s):
- Personal or unknown?
- Informal or formal?
- An "off-the-record" speaker or a "tough nut"?

G. Editor suggests strategy:
- Prepare by studying subject
- Review the knowns
- Confirm available information
- Identify the best sources of information

H. Editor assesses progress:
- Kill or pursue story
- Revise scope
- Reassign if necessary to maintain copy flow

II. Production Process: The scheduling and production of *Food & Drug Packaging* is handled at HBJ's Duluth, Minnesota, Operations Department.

A. Preparing for production:
- Proofread galleys
- Cut up galleys for paste-up into pages
- Categorize stories—
  - Up front or back of book?
  - News
  - Features
  - New products
  - Captions
  - Literature (informational material offered by advertisers and other suppliers) etc.

B. Production:
- Review "thumbnail" imposition sheet with publisher and production manager
- Plan editorial placement
- Check dummy pages against imposition sheet

- Paste up stories—
  - Accuracy is essential
  - Attention to details
  - Check conflict with ads
  - Check column widths of ads
  - Check jump lines (lines continued from one page to another)
- C. Working page proofs:
  - Write heads to proper character count
  - Transfer corrections from galleys onto page proofs
  - Reread page proofs
  - Write captions, subheads, etc.
  - Crop photographs and art
  - Final check of corrected page makeups (reproduction proofs) showing pictures in place. Send reproduction proofs to be photographed, after which film is transported to printer who prints, binds, and mails.
- D. Postmortem (basically staff discussion and editor critique)
- E. Start cycle again.

While this outline is fairly detailed, a comprehensive description of all that is involved in producing a magazine could fill an entire book (and there are books on magazine production to prove it). However, this and the short descriptions of the periodicals that follow provide a general picture of specialized business magazine planning and production.

Next a standard-size monthly magazine is discussed.

Administrative Management

Administrative Management, published by Geyer-McAllister Publications, Inc., New York, is produced by four full-time editors plus five contributing editors who submit articles on a regular basis. The magazine's art director also works on other company publications. The audited circulation of the magazine (mostly paid subscriptions) is 52,000. Printed on a sheet-fed offset press, *Administrative Management* averages 100 standard-size pages per issue (overall size 8 1/8 by 11 inches; copy area 7 by 10 inches).

Administrative Management is directed to administrative executives who are responsible for a wide variety of systems and services within their organizations, including accounting, bookkeeping, and record-keeping; data processing and word processing; telecommunications; reprographics; mail handling; and all types of allied operations. It is not addressed to all of the general interests of management, but focuses instead on the equipment and personnel needs of administration. As such, it is not an "office management" magazine, but emphasizes how systems, policies, and trends affect the overall organization.

Articles contributed to *Administrative Management* typically range between 500 and 2,000 words. They are screened for relevance, clarity, and conciseness. Good articles are considered those that communicate their ideas with almost memo-like brevity, with sufficient facts and figures to provide at least bench-mark reference points, and with enough to-the-point summation so as not to try a reader's patience.

About 25 percent of editorial content is derived from outside sources, from business managers, authorities in various fields, management theorists, and others.

An outline of the planning and production cycle for a typical issue of *Administrative Management* has been prepared by the editor/editorial director, and is divided into three time frames as follows:

1. Long-range planning—From three months to as much as a year and one-half before publication.
2. Short-range planning—From one and one-half to four months before publication.
3. Actual production—From one and one-half months before publication through press time.

It should be noted that the long-range planning described here is the exception, rather than the rule, with most business periodicals. Though it is the custom for most periodicals to establish an editorial program for an entire year, the actual planning of an issue usually begins no more than two to three months prior to publication.

LONG-RANGE PLANNING

During this period, the editorial director schedules certain key features, two or three per issue, that will appear in given issues over the upcoming 12 to 18 months. These include, for example, articles on major equipment which require extensive research. This type of planning enables the staff, well in advance, to compile files of information on the scheduled topics—for later use by the writers—and to be on the lookout for good photographs.

The editor or managing editor assigns the features to staff editors or outside authors early in the long-range planning phase, although this can also happen during the short-range period.

SHORT-RANGE PLANNING

Here the staff begins to round out the contents of approaching issues, adding other articles, either commissioned or to be staff-written. Each month the editor or managing editor distributes (for internal use) lists of the features scheduled for three "near-future" issues. The January listings, for example, outline the forthcoming April, May, and June issues.

In January, too, writers are chosen for any May articles not yet assigned, as well as any timely late-starters for April. With regard to major features on which the staff has been building files, the staff begins in January, with May in mind, to contact all significant sources (vendors, in the case of equipment round-up features) for their latest information. This helps assure the publication of thorough and recent coverage of the subject. In February the staff will attempt a final follow-up among sources that have not responded. A staff editor always does this work, even though the final article may be written by an outside author. A staff editor is always assigned to assist any such outsider.

Also, all copy, however generated, is always read and edited by at least two staffers.

By February, staff members are anticipating any major art needs for May covers, as well as any large charts or involved diagrams. Later, during the actual production phase, the staff will hold meetings with the art department.

Throughout the planning process, the staff is also developing what it calls its "shelf"—a bank of articles, more or less timeless in content, which are not scheduled for any particular issue and which may be used to balance a particular editorial "menu" or to fill a hole if an ad drops out at the last minute.

ACTUAL PRODUCTION

Here the staff begins to "put it all together." This phase is described in several weekly time frames. *Administrative Management* is mailed by the first of the month for which it is dated, and thus comes off press in the last days of the preceding month.

Six weeks prior to publication: Having determined the size and nature of its major features, the staff outlines for the production department its editorial "musts." The production department has responsibility for impositioning the book (the term *book* is a popular printing term for periodical). So long as the staff keeps its "must" list within reasonable bounds—where it must have a spread, where it needs a right-hand page, where it requires color—the production department has no trouble fulfilling the requests. The editorial staff, for its part, understands that certain portions of the book must be kept flexible to accommodate advertising needs—color, inserts, last-minute changes, and so on.

At this time, the editorial staff meets with the art department to "see the book as a whole" and plan any layouts not yet in the works.

Six to four weeks prior to publication: Final copy goes to the printer, including text for most of the regular departments. Product photos for the "New Equipment" section go to art for cropping.

Five to four weeks prior to publication: The staff begins what it calls "bogus dummying"—bogus because the staff does not yet have the final folios (page numbers) for the pages it is handling, and will not for another week or two. Confident that its "must" requests will be honored, however, and knowing the shape of recurring columns and pages, it can safely proceed.

In the Geyer-McAllister "shop"—unlike some publishing houses—editors do their own dummying (layout of copy). This is not unusual, though. In most medium-size periodical publishing firms, dummying is done by the editorial staff. This gives the staff greater control of the page and of the many editorial decisions that dummying entails.

Four to three weeks prior to publication: Final impositioned dummy is received from the production department. "Bogus" pages are given final folios. Early page proofs are read, corrected if necessary, and returned to the printer.

Two weeks prior to publication: Remaining page proofs are okayed; file proofs are checked and kept.

Six to four working days prior to publication: Blue lines are checked; corrections called in. The issue then goes to press.

Now to the operation of a weekly periodical, *Feedstuffs*, "the weekly newspaper for agribusiness."

Feedstuffs

Feedstuffs, a 15- by 10-inch tabloid, is published by Miller Publishing Company, Minneapolis, Minnesota (acquired by American Broadcasting Companies [ABC] in 1977). *Feedstuffs* has been a part of agriculture for over 50 years, since its founding in 1929 as a trade publication for the "feed manufacturer, feed broker, feed jobber, and feed dealer." At that time, farmers were buying $900 million in animal feed, or about 12 percent of the $7.5 billion they spent that year for all farm products and services. By 1975, feed manufacturing had become a $13 billion industry, with feed representing more than 17 percent of the $75 billion in production goods and services that keep American farms running.

Feedstuffs has changed just as dramatically. While its 22,500 weekly subscribers still include traditional feed manufacturers, grain merchants, and other companies that supply basic products or services to agriculture, *Feedstuffs'* newer readers include commercial poultry and livestock producers who sell to fast-food chains, for example. And just as agriculture has been "internationalized" by the dramatic boom in world food trade during the last ten years, *Feedstuffs*, too, has gone international, with readers in almost every country of the world.

Among the major reasons behind *Feedstuffs'* dominance in the "animal-agribusiness" industry are its unequaled achievements in providing complete and fast news coverage of the week's events in agribusiness.

In its average news hold of nearly 30 pages each week (advertising takes up about 24 pages), *Feedstuffs* presents material ranging from commodity market news to technical articles on nutrition. Published every Friday, the publication arrives on most readers' desks the following Monday morning, making it a dependable source of information not only for the leaders in the industry, but also for consultants, financial leaders, legislators, government regulators, educators, and others.

The staff consists of eight full-time editors and more than 20 market reporters and correspondents around the nation. A Brussels correspondent also reports on agribusiness in Europe. The thousands of reports funneled into this staff are boiled down each week to about 50,000 words that take the average subscriber 45 minutes to read. Each copy of *Feedstuffs* is read by about three persons, bringing the weekly audience to nearly 65,000 readers.

Editorial planning for *Feedstuffs* is both ongoing and long-term. Each November and December the editor and his staff revise the publication's annual editorial plan for the following year. That plan takes into account the total editorial pages allocated (based on the amount of advertising budgeted), the space needed for news versus that for feature articles, the profile and the business interests of readers, and the results of ongoing readership studies. While the plan sets the average number of pages by general subject per issue, the pages devoted to any topic in a single week will, of course, vary.

The news hold in the final 20 page "form," or "signature," printed each Friday is reserved for late-breaking news stories. The other editorial pages are filled with the 15 regular weekly departments on management, research, personnel, and marketing topics, as well as with two or three major feature articles on animal nutrition, production, management, and market trends.

Twelve issues each year of *Feedstuffs* highlight special segments of the readership, emphasizing topics such as feed formulation, finance, management, grain merchandising, advertising, livestock and poultry nutrition, and international marketing. In addition, *Feedstuffs'* "Reference Issue," published as a fifty-third issue, features annual marketing statistics, nutrition and health guidelines, feed-milling information, and a buyers' guide.

Two weeks before publication, the staff in Minneapolis writes and edits feature articles as well as those ongoing departments that are to be printed first each week. Copy is sent to the typesetter (an outside firm) as it is ready, and galley proofs of advance material are then returned to the editors.

With many of the stories thus underway, the editorial staff meets each Tuesday morning to give final shape to the week's issue. The editor maintains daily telephone contact with a Washington office, where two full-time editors cover Congress, the White House, regulatory agencies, and various trade associations. (The Washington staff assumed greater responsibility beginning in the 1970's, as government regulations mushroomed and Congress has been in session nearly year-round.)

The job of covering agribusiness outside of Washington has also changed considerably in recent years. Many companies have expanded into new food ventures and diversified. And more of *Feedstuffs'* readers now specialize in only one aspect of their company's business, a fact that has led the staff itself to specialize more, with individual editors assigned to specific beats: commodities, marketing, livestock, poultry and agriculture, or fish farming. In addition to covering day-to-day developments, each editor spends part of each month traveling to industry meetings and seminars or developing feature articles about front-runners in the industry.

Working from rough layouts provided by the editor (for feature articles) and by the managing editor (for news stories), a production assistant pastes up a rough dummy of each page, using galley proofs of type. These dummies are routed through the editorial staff members, who read the copy for any changes or typographical errors before returning it to the typesetter for final paste-up.

By 5:00 p.m. on Friday, the editorial staff gives a final check to the news pages (the last pages to be readied for the printer). By 8:00 p.m., the web offset presses are rolling. Soon after, the printed forms are returned to *Feedstuffs*, where the company's own bindery binds, labels, and delivers the tabloid to the local post office and to the Minneapolis airport. *Feedstuffs* has "newspaper" mailing privileges, permitting it to move as rapidly as first-class mail. Except for those airmailed to Amsterdam, copies going to 2,500 other international readers travel by surface mail.

Restaurant Business

Restaurant Business, formerly known as *Fast Foods*, is a leading monthly magazine covering the entire restaurant field, including "fast food" operations. It is a standard-size 8 1/2- by 11-inch publication, published by Bill Communications, Inc., New York. The editorial staff consists of an editor and five assistants, plus a number of specialists.

Restaurant Business is planned in two sections: The main editorial feature of the month—the cover story—is planned months in advance because it demands considerable research and writing time. The other section, also prepared ahead of the other articles, is the food section. This feature is developed by the food editor in consultation with the editor, and general topics are agreed upon for a 12-month period.

In September, a general staff meeting is held to help plan the cover stories for the first six months of the coming year. At this meeting, decisions are made on the most important issues facing the food service industry, topics of interest to readers are discussed, and the restaurants selected for coverage in upcoming months are reviewed.

Once the general topics have been identified, article formats and approaches are decided upon. Editors are then assigned stories and given sources to contact.

For the sake of immediacy, research and writing of articles generally begins no more than two months before publication. All four-color editorial matter (approximately 30 percent of the book) is due at the printer seven weeks before publication. The art director prepares a rough layout for each story after conferring with the managing editor. Some stories work best with photographs, while others need some other form of illustration, such as cartoons or drawings. The final decision is the joint function of the art and editorial departments.

Cover ideas are discussed by the editor and the art director, the managing editor, and the writer assigned to the story. After the art concept is agreed upon, only the managing editor will work with the art director. This simplifies follow-through procedures and frees the editor to concentrate on the story.

Articles are written, are given to the editor for approval, and then go to the managing editor for editing. The title, decks, and captions are written at the same time. Manuscripts begin to go to the typesetter six weeks before publication. When galleys are returned from the typesetter, the managing editor and an editor who did not write the story do the proofreading. Pasteups and mechanicals are prepared in the art department.

The production schedule is as follows:

1. All manuscripts are sent to the typesetter over a five-day period beginning six weeks prior to publication.
2. At this time, the managing editor submits to the art and production departments an editorial breakdown for each story, showing number of pages requested, special positions (spreads, right-hand page, etc.), and color requirements.
3. Galleys are returned from the typesetter within three working days. Editors then proofread the returned galleys.
4. During that time, the final page count of the magazine is decided, based on a ratio of editorial pages to number of ads.
5. The art department begins to paste up mechanicals five weeks before the month of issue, completing this work over a five-day period.
6. Pasteups go to the managing editor for approval.

7. Pasteups are then sent to the printer.
8. Page proofs are returned from the printer for okay by the art department and managing editor, and are then returned over a five-day period.
9. Ozalids (or blues) are returned from the printer and approved over the phone by the art department and managing editor.
10. The issue goes to press.
11. The magazine is mailed on the twenty-second day of the month preceding date of issue.

Articles by columnists that appear monthly in *Restaurant Business* are planned jointly by the columnists and their respective editors. General topics are planned in advance, but if a more important subject arises, it takes precedence in the column.

The food section is on a different schedule from the other stories. It runs from six to eight pages each month, and includes three or four pictures along with menu-merchandising ideas. This section is written by the food editor, who is a trained and experienced chef. Three months before publication, the food editor and the editor decide on the exact food items to be presented, pick the appropriate photographic "props," and (in conjunction with the art director and the food photographer) plan the shots to be used. The food editor prepares the food in the test kitchen, and it is photographed in the magazine's own studio.

Although the editor of *Restaurant Business* believes in the importance of advance article planning, even cover stories are scrapped or downgraded if they do not ultimately reflect current needs, problems, and opportunities.

Business Periodicals: Demonstrating Leadership

It is hoped that the above descriptions have provided readers with a fairly comprehensive picture of what happens behind the scenes of specialized magazines. The business magazine student and beginning journalist may wish to obtain copies of the four periodicals discussed, as well as other specialized business periodicals, for review and study.

Clearly, no set methodology is used by the above-described publications to plan, write, edit, and produce the final product. Each is a high-quality and timely periodical. In this connection, it is important to mention that because of the high standards developed by business periodical journalism over the years, the finished product is usually equal in quality and often superior to the best of consumer magazines. Yet, with few exceptions, the staffs and budgets of business periodicals are usually smaller than those of consumer magazines. Business periodical editing and publishing has reached such a degree of maturity and excellence that one has to search far to locate bad journalism. Of course, some still exists, but to a much lesser extent than in the consumer magazine field.

The years 1977 through 1982 saw a record number of magazine start-ups, both business and consumer, despite the continued growth and popularity of broadcast and other forms of electronic media.

One reason why comparatively more new business periodicals than consumer magazines have survived is the high journalistic standards established in the specialized business periodical field, in which magazines staffed by expert writers and editors cater to markets with specific informational needs. Most of the business periodicals launched in the last five years have responded to the new technological developments of industry, such as new forms of computers. Most of the recent new consumer magazines that have succeeded have also been in specialized areas, such as sports (tennis and jogging magazines have developed a large following) and other forms of recreation. In my view, many consumer magazines have not succeeded because they failed to set and follow good standards of journalism.

The business press, then, by its standards of excellence, exerts leadership in the entire magazine industry; in addition, business editors also have an opportunity to become spokespersons and to gain recognition in the industries they serve. For example, in addition to deciding the content of an issue, which in itself provides readers with a sense of an industry's direction, editors often use their columns to discuss unexplored and sometimes controversial issues. Sometimes such columns lead to productive action by the industry involved. Gone is the day when business periodicals merely reported news or offered "how to" articles; more and more the "why" is being emphasized.

Other ways that business periodical editors exert leadership are through their participation in the development of seminars; in ongoing contacts with industry executives; and in assisting in the planning of convention programs and regional meetings. The specialized business periodical editor today is truly in a position to be a leader of the business community served by his or her publication.

An "Untypical" Day in the Life of an Editor

To document the multi-faceted activities of the "editor at work," about a dozen editors of various specialized business publications were asked to describe their "typical" work day. The result? There is no such thing! If there is a common denominator at all, it is the almost endless number of different problems, challenges, and creative opportunities provided by their jobs. Though there is no "typical" day as such, a number of duties, tasks, and events usually occur each day.

An editor who has risen through the ranks typically finds that more and more time is taken up by "paper shuffling," meetings, supervisory functions, and public relations—all of which draw him or her away from the "real" work of writing and producing a publication. By hiring competent staff members and by learning to delegate, however, editors can still schedule their time so that they are involved in the day-to-day work of the publication.

The following description, not without elements of hyperbole, singles out some of the frustrating and fulfilling—but rarely dull—moments of a journalist's day.

The Mail . . . Mondays are always the worst. Three or four issues of *The Federal Register* must be pored through in search of potential stories. A foot-high pile of press releases, literature, and story submissions must be analyzed for suitability and then sorted and assigned to various editors or departments. Some stories say "see enclosed photograph" and there is none. Some photographs arrive mysteriously with no accompanying story. There are invitations to press briefings, luncheons, and an occasional gala product introduction. Then there are the "letters to the editor"—with praise and damnation, but mostly asking "where can I buy a. . . ." Competitors' issues arrive, and you cringe as you open them, hoping there won't be any surprises.

The Telephone . . . always rings just when you don't have time to talk. And on the busiest days it rings the most. Telephone calls fall into three categories: (1) Good News—"We loved the story. It was a real service to the industry. Can we buy reprints?" (2) Bad News—"Your story contained three unforgivable errors"; or "This is the printer. Our presses broke and your issue will be late"; or "This is the photo lab. We lost your order"; or "This is the receptionist—the gentleman out here doesn't have an appointment, but he says he'll only take a few minutes of your time"; (3) The Question—"Where can I buy a . . . ?"; or "This is 'Freeloaders Journal.' Can you tell me everything that has happened in your industry over the last five years? My deadline is three o'clock." Or "Can you give us a couple hours of free consulting?"

The Real Work . . . Every day begins with a delivery (you hope) from the printer. Such copy usually requires an hour or more of proofreading or examination. Ad proofs and film also arrive and must be sorted out and taken to the production department.

After the mail and printer's delivery are dispensed with, you go about producing something to return to the printer that afternoon. This may mean writing stories or dummying pages for the next issue. The writing may involve lengthy telephone calls to research the story or extensive rewriting of a submitted article, or both. It's difficult to be creative when the phones are ringing and people are coming in and out of the office. Therefore, you often take work home at night, or occasionally work at home. Sometimes, too, a story begins with a visit to a plant or facility to see the operation in action; such visits account for several days a month for some journalists.

When it comes to preparing article layouts, several departments of the company work together. The size of the issue is discussed with the production department, as well as any special requirements. Special layouts are assigned to the art department, which is also consulted on choice of photographs, use of color, typefaces and logos, placement and balance of items on a page, plus any required charts or diagrams. With other staff members, you discuss which stories to emphasize, which to downplay, which to hold for another issue. You spend the afternoon editing, or perhaps dummying, experiencing an extra surge of adrenalin as the printer's pickup time approaches.

The Rewards . . . The ultimate goal is to get the issue out on time, while maintaining the highest possible quality. Somewhere in the middle are the compromises that any job entails. The continuing thrill of seeing a story in print on which you have worked hard and which you feel will be well received is a form of immediate satisfaction that does not exist in many other professions.

If you are a biweekly editor, you have to churn out a product so often that routine tasks may no longer move you; sometimes it takes a special effort to keep the juices flowing. What you may be forgetting is that a story that is mundane to you can still be exciting to the reader if it involves his or her company or product or provides information he or she needs to know.

As an editor of a specialized business magazine, you must have an almost intuitive sense that allows you to correct for drift from the printing schedule and to concentrate on essentials (again, getting the magazine out on time with the "latest and the best"), while also keeping many other balls in the air.

How do editors feel about their jobs? In my opinion, C. S. Cronan, long-time editor of *Chemical Engineering*, spoke for many other editors in his acceptance speech on receiving the 1981 American Business Press's Crain Award (given for outstanding career achievement). His comments, in part, follow:

"My initial reaction to receiving this award is that I would really like to start my career all over again because being a business paper editor has been so satisfying.

"Why do I feel this way? To begin with, we're in business to help other people do their jobs better. You might say we reduce or relieve frustrations by giving our readers information that will help them solve problems. Contrast that, if you will, with the popular media that seem to generate and feed frustrations.

"As we go about developing and publishing helpful, job-related information for our reading audiences, we enjoy the unparalleled good fortune to be dealing with a constantly changing scene. How could anyone in our business lack for interesting and exciting situations to unravel for our readers? After all, we're dealing with portions of a national economy that produced a total GNP of $2.626 trillion in 1980. By tracking the dynamics of our particular portions day by day, we regularly uncover important developments and place them in perspective. In that way, we exert a strong influence on the future.

"How well we carry out these activities can profoundly affect the fortunes of our readers and their companies. Those of us who do it well earn increasing respect and loyalty. Those who do it poorly lose readers and competitive position.

"There is a parallel benefit to performing well. Good performance begets profit for our publishing companies. And out of that profit comes funding for expansion into other information services. Our companies and their employees grow in stature and rewards, and the users of our services acquire more knowledge to propel their businesses into new areas of growth and productivity.

"Looking to the future, it seems we must all outdo our previous efforts. American business and industry no longer enjoy preeminent positions in many national as well as world markets. To remain fully competitive and regain some of the leads once held will require improved foresight and determination. Most certainly, we in the business press face the challenge of providing leadership. That will mean an all-out drive to become more creative, more persistent, more productive, and more convincing in developing and delivering information that will help build the future strength of the companies we serve."

CHAPTER 6

Basic Economics/Organization and Budgeting/Departmental Functions

BASIC ECONOMICS

The basic goals of a business periodical publishing company are no different from those of any other business—to make a fair profit and to grow. However, the means used to accomplish these aims differ from those of other business enterprises, and relate to the fact that specialized periodical publishing is creative and constantly changing.

Products and Services

Though classified as a service industry, business periodical publishers produce *both products* and *services*. Products include periodicals; directories, manuals, and buying guides; newsletters; books; seminars; and trade shows.

The basic service that the publisher provides is information—usually in-depth and highly specialized. Marketing, usually direct-mail marketing, is another service. Marketing involves mailings to individuals on a magazine's circulation list to promote books, newsletters, and other corporation products. With few exceptions such lists are computerized; they are usually available on a demographic basis. Ordinarily one cannot buy the list but only the limited right to use it.

Profit Centers

The specialized activities within a company are usually divided into profit centers, with a group publisher or publishing manager in charge of each. Typically, a profit-center chief has had (or obtained) some financial training and experience, in addition to is or her specialized business experience. In medium-size and smaller companies, the services mentioned earlier become part of the profit centers of group publishers, especially publishers who function under the decentralized system, explained later in this chapter.

Each head of a profit center develops a well-defined budget, which is approved and reviewed by management periodically, usually once a month. In most instances, a profit-center manager heads a group of specialized magazines that have a common denominator, such as subject area focus. He or she also directs the operations of all other products and services related to the fields covered. The chief thus presides over a complete range of products and services dealing with a special field of interest, related industries, or segments of industries.

In some companies, especially among larger corporations, a more specialized approach may be used. Thus, a group publisher may direct a profit center that includes only magazines and allied products such as directories, while books, encompassing the fields of all the periodicals published by the company, may be operated as a separate unit and profit center. The same may be true for newsletters and manuals, and for the operation of trade shows.

Cash Flow

The publishing of specialized business periodicals and production of ancillary products and services is a "cash" business, but it is not "cash-intensive," meaning that captial investments are normally minimal. For example, the only major equipment purchased may include in-house computerized typesetting equipment and computers. The cost of such machines is relatively modest and the eventual savings can be great. Often, leasing arrangements are made. Although the use of in-house electronic typesetting is increasing, at this writing (1983) only a minority of publishing companies have such equipment.

More specifically, business periodical publishing is a cash business because it is only after a magazine is produced that the company receives bills for services rendered, including those for printing and binding (by far the biggest item of cost outside of salaries) as well as those from the fulfillment company (which maintains the circulation list) and other service organizations. At the same time, invoices to the magazine's advertisers are mailed immediately upon publication of the magazine, so that the positive cash flow starts within 10 days after this billing. Within a month (or two), most of the advertising dollars have been received. It is then that the printing and other major bills are normally paid. Under normal economic conditions, publishing a successful business periodical provides a healthy cash flow, and bank loans for operational purposes are rarely needed. During the 1980-1982 recession, however, advertising agencies often took 60 to 90 days, or more, to pay their bills, resulting in cash-flow problems for publishers.

Publishers do need ready cash (aside from salaries and bill paying) to make cash deposits with the post office to cover mailing costs and to buy paper on which to print the magazines (unless the printer provides it).

Salaries and Departmental Costs

Business periodical publishing is not cash-intensive, but it is labor-intensive. Aside from mechanical and distribution costs (printing, paper, binding, and mailing), salaries represent the single biggest expense. For example, on average, a company publishing from six to twelve magazines with an annual net revenue of $10 million will have a payroll of approximately $2 1/2 million. With some exceptions, publishers of business periodicals pay their employees twice a month. Most have company-paid pension or profit-sharing programs, as well as health and group insurance plans, funded mostly (or entirely) by the company.

All departmental salaries, except those of the publishers and the sales staff, are fixed. In other words, the editorial, accounting, production, art, and circulation departments, plus all other employees, are paid a set salary, with periodic merit increases. The publisher, who heads a profit center, receives a fixed salary plus a percentage based on any improvement in the contribution to overhead of his or her profit center. This percentage varies with the company, but the normal range is five to ten percent. Salespersons are paid on the basis of a salary or "bogey," which represents the amount of advertising income they are given to service, plus a commission on new and additional advertising sold.

After the mechanical and distribution costs and payroll, advertising and promotion—largely salaries, incentives, and travel and entertainment (T & E) expenses—constitute the next largest item of cost, followed by editorial costs, circulation costs, and "other direct expenses." ("Other direct expenses" represent elements such as *pro rata* rent; management salaries and managers' T & E; and accounting—prorated on actual use on behalf of the magazines and other products and services.)

CIRCULATION COSTS

During the past few years, circulation costs have been increasing, both in terms of payroll expenses and fulfillment charges. For magazines with basically paid circulation, the cost of obtaining and maintaining paid subscriptions has increased substantially since the late 1970s, and will continue to do so. However, the maintenance of controlled lists (the type of circulation chosen by most business periodicals) has also shown major cost increases over the years. This is largely the result of more sophisticated and intensified approaches used to build and maintain circulation. For example, most (by far) controlled magazines now offer "request circulation." This means distribution of a magazine to a reader who has actually requested it. To maintain a request circulation for one or even two years has become costly: Form letters to readers and potential readers must be mailed in a series, sometimes three or more times before sufficient numbers respond.

This is done on a continuing basis. In some cases, request circulation can cost more than paid circulation, the difference being that paid circulation is controlled with lists of readers who are most likely to buy the product or services. Such lists have been carefully selected over a period of time; the experience is that people whose names are on such lists have continued to subscribe to specialized business magazines.

Since 1980, mailing costs have continued to escalate, largely because of sharp postal rate increases. Regular, periodic increases can be anticipated. And while postal rates have increased, mailing services have deteriorated. Paid circulation periodicals no longer receive special postal treatment. Except for daily and some newspaper-type weeklies, which receive special "newspaper" delivery service, it takes two weeks or longer for most magazines to be delivered.

As a result of high postal rates and other mailing costs, subscription prices have been raised substantially, some to as high as $50 or more per year. Foreign subscription prices have also been increased considerably.

More newly launched business periodicals survive and thrive than do new consumer magazines. One of the major reasons for this, aside from their greater "fix" on their readers, is that the costs of starting and running a business periodical are considerably less than are those for a consumer magazine. One basic factor is circulation. Whereas the circulation of a consumer magazine can run from a low of 100,000 to a high in the millions, that of a business periodical is in the thousands. Some of the most successful and profitable business magazines, for example, have circulations ranging between 20,000 and 50,000. And a few flourish with 10,000 or less. Exceptions (over 50,000 circulation) are found among professional magazines, especially medical journals. But even there, magazines covering the total market are few: most medical journals represent subspecialties of surgery, urology, family practice, and neurology.

The circulation of a business periodical depends on the size of the market covered, including the number of plants and other establishments related to the industry or profession, and the number of potential readers. This is known as the *universe* of the market. Owing to continuing mergers and acquisitions, the number of corporations in many industries is becoming smaller, and plants are becoming larger but fewer. In other words, the universe (of readers) of most industries continues to contract. The goal, then, must be to attain numbers of readers, as opposed to simply one or a few, per plant.

Unlike consumer magazines, which generally have paid subscriptions, most business periodicals attain readership by means of controlled circulation, which is a sophisticated way of gaining qualified readers. Controlled circulation is accomplished as follows: The publisher of a magazine that covers the computer field, for example, first develops a list which represents the universe of readers; it includes manufacturers of both hard- and software and computer users. The publisher can purchase such lists from list-selling firms or obtain them from trade associations and professional organizations. After the list is compiled, it is categorized into types of readers—by size of company, function of reader in management (such as chief executive officer, equipment buyer, director of marketing, etc.), location (such as state or country), and often by more elaborated classifications. Typically, the publishers will also carefully compare their circulation with that of major competing periodicals.

Most established business periodicals are audited by either the BPA (Business Publications Audit of Circulation, Inc.) or the ABC (Audit Bureau of Circulations). Until several years ago, the ABC audited only paid publications (its major business still consists of auditing consumer magazines and daily newspapers). However, today it audits nonpaid or controlled circulation business periodicals as well. If the bulk of the circulation of a business magazine is nonpaid, the ABC requires that 50 percent of the circulation represent "request circulation."

The BPA, which has many more business magazines among its membership than the ABC, also audits (though it does not require) "request circulation." It does insist that the business magazines it audits have qualified readers who are verifiable. Both audit bureaus attempt to ensure credibility of circulation or potential readership. Because of competitive pressures (and the specific needs of some advertisers and their agencies) more and more publishers are moving in the direction of one-year "request circulation." The ABC and the BPA are working together to achieve industry comparability standards. Under this program, magazines covering the same market develop a system by which to compare the classification of readers, thus enabling advertisers to more precisely compare the circulation of periodicals. (More on this later in the chapter.) Most magazines audited by the ABC or the BPA also conduct readership studies (often by hiring an agency). Advertisers or their agencies also sometimes do their own readership studies.

The costs of circulation and readership studies can be substantial and become part of a magazine's total circulation and distribution budget. (Audits are discussed in more detail later in this chapter under the description of circulation department functions.)

ADVERTISING RATES

Advertising rates are based upon the total costs of producing and distributing the periodical, plus a markup for profit. Because of cost increases in all areas in recent years, publishers' rate increases are often now semiannual instead of annual.

In determining a magazine's budget and profitability, careful thought must be given to the percentage of advertising pages, as compared to editorial pages, in an average issue. The general rule of thumb is "60-40" or at least "55-45," meaning 60 percent (or 55 percent) advertising, as against 40 percent (or 45 percent) editorial. Though such percentages can and do vary, experience has shown that it is difficult to show the needed profit when a publication has less than 50 percent of its pages in paid advertising.

How many advertising pages are needed to break even in a new business magazine? This depends on many variables—the type of periodical, the circulation needed, the market to be covered, and whether the new periodical is launched by an established publishing company or by a single entrepreneur. Experience has shown that for a new magazine of 48 to 60 pages, and with circulation no higher than 20,000, the minimum number of advertising pages per issue needed to break even (or even approach it) is 20. This applies to an operation that is launched by an entrepreneurial editor or sales executive who has a knowledge of the field and can keep costs to a minimum. Naturally, a larger circulation or a greater number of pages would require a higher minimum number of advertising pages per issue.

While magazine publishing costs have increased substantially in recent years, the overall economic outlook for publishing business periodicals continues to be positive. This is largely the result of greater acceptance of business magazines by the advertising community, not only as vital sources of communication that generate advertising inquiries and eventual orders for materials and equipment, but as image-builders for supply firms of all types.

The Profession of Selling Advertising

Selling advertising for a business magazine has become a profession. No longer does the advertising salesperson sell merely by making old-fashioned "goodwill calls." He or she must now visit every advertiser and good prospect at least two to six times a year, in addition to calling upon advertising agency media buyers and account executives. Such calls entail well-planned presentations—dealing with circulation, market penetration, readership, and other tangible forms of information of value to the advertiser—and sometimes, also, special information of direct, practical value (such as the knowledge that a major food manufacturer is planning to build a new plant and will require certain kinds of equipment).

What the advertiser expects for his or her advertising dollars are maximum exposure and increased product sales. Given the high quality of most of today's business and professional magazines, the former is usually not difficult to obtain.

To help the advertiser receive reader inquiries on products, most business periodicals today provide a reader service card bound into all issues. The reader service card enables readers to request information about products and services offered by the magazine's advertisers, as well as information about specific items mentioned in the issue (such as those included in the New Literature/New Products departments). Reader service cards are normally mailed by readers to the publication headquarters or to a computer center. After tallying and analyzing the cards, the publication then sends them to the advertisers and other suppliers.

Providing a reader service card represents an expense to the publishers, but it has proved valuable both to advertisers and publishers. For advertisers, the card can mean increased sales; and for publishers, it serves as an extra inducement for an advertiser. Also, information from the cards can be used in sales presentations. In addition, some suppliers included on the reader service card eventually become advertisers.

Economics of Medical Magazines

In discussing the economics of specialized business periodicals, special mention must be given to medical magazines, the largest single group of professional publications. There are approximately 350 medical magazines, most covering subspecialties and disciplines. Pharmaceutical firms, by far the major advertisers, invest close to $300 million in these journals. Nevertheless, the cost of publishing a medical magazine is much higher than that of publishing an industrial periodical.

There are several reasons for this: First, a substantial percentage of medical magazines have fairly large circulations, ranging from 50,000 to over 250,000, despite the fact that more and more medical journals are concentrating on narrow specialties, rather than seeking total-market concentration. In order to reach *all* physicians in practice, for example, a medical journal would need a circulation close to 300,000. Though few medical magazines have such a circulation, a fair number do reach over 200,000 physicians in private and hospital practice; these are called "mass-circulation" periodicals. A second group with large circulations are called "mini-mass" magazines; these reach general practitioners, family practitioners, internists, and osteopaths, and have circulations ranging from 80,000 to 120,000. Given such high circulations, the cost of printing, binding, and mailing a medical journal far exceeds most industrial magazines.

A second reason for the high publishing costs of medical

journals is that advertising rates in this field are much lower in proportion to copies printed and mailed than are those of industrial publications. Medical advertising rates are (generally) based on cost per 1,000 copies of the journal, while rates of industrial periodicals are normally based on percent of market coverage or penetration. For example, industrial magazines with a circulation of 50,000, but with significant market penetration, might have a one-time rate per page of $3,500 to $4,000 or higher. On the other hand a medical magazine with a mini-mass circulation of 120,000 might have a page rate of about $2,000 or less.

In this connection it should be mentioned that about 30 pharmaceutical companies account for the production and marketing of the great percentage of prescription drugs. But each of these companies markets a variety of so-called "ethical," or "substitute," prescription drug products, with the result that many of the 30 will use multi-page advertising campaigns in many medical journals—from 4 to 24 per issue—to publicize these products. Such a practice is both good and bad for medical journals: Good, because advertising sales personnel can concentrate on a small number of advertisers, most located in a single marketing area such as suburban New Jersey; and bad, because rates per page are rendered much lower than the 1-time or even 12-time rate (some pharmaceutical firms will run as many as 96 advertising pages per year in several magazines). As a result, medical magazines may have rates on a scale from 24 to 96 insertions per year.

Medical magazine costs are higher in just about all other areas. For example, medical magazine editors and advertising salespersons are the highest paid in the business periodical field, some earning $50,000 to $75,000 per year. (Editors and advertising personnel of industrial publications, with some exceptions, earn about $35,000 to $50,000 per year).

Launching a new medical magazine also involves a higher investment. While an industrial periodical can break even within a three-year period, it often takes five years or longer for a medical magazine to reach profitability. This is because competition is much keener, and pharmaceutical firms are less apt than industrial advertisers to advertise in a new magazine. Often pharmaceutical firms will wait three years before advertising in a new medical magazine. But there are exceptions, especially in highly specialized periodicals, edited and/or published by people who have recognized experience and reputations in medical publishing. This brings up another unique factor in medical periodical publishing. Pharmaceutical advertisers buy space in a periodical based on "numbers"—numbers of readers surveyed in recognized readership studies in the field, as well as numbers selected by advertisers themselves. Such "numbers" often include advertising rates and the extent of market coverage needed for certain products. What such figures and other market models show can often make or break a medical magazine.

Although the "downside" risks are much higher in the medical field than for industrial publications, the potential for growth and profitability is also much higher. Several medical magazines have advertising revenue of $10 million to $20 million a year, and those with annual advertising sales of $3 million to $5 million are the rule. Few industrial magazines, however, reach annual advertising sales of $3 million to $5 million.

ORGANIZATION AND BUDGETING

The following section discusses the overall organization of a business periodical publishing company and the budgeting and general functions of each department.

While various multi-publication publishers may follow different systems of producing their periodicals, the basic style of organization may be described as either centralized or decentralized.

Decentralized Organization

The majority of multi-publication publishers (especially those that are public corporations or divisions of these) follow the decentralized plan. In a decentralized organization, a publisher of one magazine or a group publisher of several periodicals operates his or her unit as if it were a personal business—but according to specific parameters established by management and subject to management supervision, review, and guidance.

Management usually consists of: (l) the chairman and chief executive officer; (2) the president and chief administrative officer; (3) an editorial director, who normally is a vice president; (4) the controller or chief financial officer, who is vice president and/or treasurer (or just the latter); and (5) a vice president in charge of sales and marketing. The various departments of a decentralized organization normally include: editorial, production, circulation, art, and advertising or accounting. Each department has a manager and staff as required. Many decentralized operations also have a vice president in charge of purchasing, who directs the buying of printing, paper, and other supplies, often in conjunction with departmental heads. Following is a description of the major responsibilities of the management team.

The chairman and chief executive officer determines policy and keeps in touch with the operations of all of the company magazines—by regular meetings with the president; by reviewing all of the magazines as they come off the press; in periodic meetings with group publishers; and by regular contact with the chief accounting officer on cash flow, billing, and collections. He or she is particularly involved in mergers and acquisitions and in the development of new products.

The president and chief administrator supervises the work of all departments and meets regularly with department heads.

The vice president and editorial director supervises the editorial work of all periodicals, is often involved in hiring editorial staff, and meets regularly with editors to review and discuss editorial problems and to set goals for editorial excellence.

BUDGETING PROCEDURES

The publisher, as manager of his or her unit, begins to formulate the annual budget in late summer or early fall for the following calendar year. If the corporation uses a fiscal-year approach, budget planning begins from six months to a minimum of three months prior to the beginning of the fiscal year.

Prior to budget planning, a member of the management team, such as (in smaller companies) the chairman and chief executive officer or the president and chief administrative officer, will send publishers a memo outlining budget parameters and special needs for the year ahead. In some cases, discussion on key points will also take place between the publisher and management personnel.

Once the budget goals are set, the publisher (the manager of the periodical(s) under his or her jurisdiction) begins the work of developing a preliminary budget, usually in the following manner: A detailed form is mailed to the salespersons, asking them to project the number of advertising pages anticipated from their territories in the year ahead. The editor in chief of each publication is also asked for his or her budgetary needs. At the same time, the publisher meets with the heads of the circulation, production, and art departments to determine their projected costs. Finally, he or she meets with the chief accounting officer or the officer's assistant to clear and/or confirm the various cost elements that are to be included in the budget.

Having received all needed data and having consulted with the accounting department, the publisher formulates the preliminary budget. Normally, management will expect actual results to be within 5 percent or less of the submitted and approved budgets. Thus, "blue sky" projections (whether by salespersons or other departments) can be dangerous and should be altered by the publisher. With some exceptions, the range of "contributions to overhead" (a term used to denote profits before several administrative costs, taxes, and other special items) in the specialized periodical business is 10 to 20 percent, thus resulting in a net profit after taxes ranging from 5 to 10 percent. Such profit results can vary with a particular publication because of special competitive situations, extraordinary expenses needed to boost circulation, and the general economy. The best-managed companies, which have seasoned periodicals with fairly high advertising volume (from $2 million to $10 million annually per publication), show a better than 10 percent contribution to overhead. Less successful companies, especially those with smaller magazines (annual advertising revenue of $1 million or less per publication) will show a contribution to overhead of less than 10 percent.

The preliminary budget is then submitted to the accounting department, which checks all figures and incorporates general and administrative as well as needed indirect departmental costs for each publication. (The latter items represent portions of general departmental costs, such as rent, salaries, and numerous other costs prorated for each publication.)

The chief accounting officer will meet with the publisher to review and discuss the completed preliminary budget. The chief accounting officer then presents the publisher's preliminary budget (plus the budgets of the other publishing groups) to both the president and the chairman.

Following review of the preliminary budget by the chairman and president, both will meet with the chief accounting officer to discuss any item in question. They then meet with each publisher for a final review. At this point, final questions are asked and adjustments made as needed. The budgets are then returned to the chief accounting officer, who, with his or her staff, includes all needed changes, adds a summary, and then submits the final corporate budget (and divisional "breakouts") to the president and chairman for approval. Once the budget is approved, a copy is presented to each publisher.

MONTHLY REVENUES

While management reviews monthly results (submitted by the chief accounting officer) to compare them with the current monthly budget and the previous year's monthly figures, no changes are made (except under unusual circumstances) in the total annual budget. If the monthly and quarterly results are substantially lower than the budgetary figures, management will meet with the publisher to determine reasons for such discrepancies and to offer suggestions to the publisher for needed cost reductions for the months to follow. In most instances, monthly, and especially quarterly, results do not differ by more than 5 percent from budgetary figures. However, alert publishers should be aware of and advise management of anticipated problems.

The publisher and/or the accounting department also normally provides relevant portions of monthly budget results to departmental heads. The editorial director and the corporate sales manager are thus given the opportunity to review editorial and advertising and promotional parts of the budgets.

Centralized Organization

Under the centralized system of operation, magazine publishers are only indirectly involved in determining profitability of the publication under their direction. The basic function of the publisher of a centralized operation is to produce a magazine (or magazines) of quality with the greatest number of advertising pages. His or her incentive, in terms of personal income, is a program of remuneration based on an increased number of advertising pages and advertising dollars as compared with the previous year.

In planning a budget, the publisher of a centralized system follows the same methodology in determining the number of advertising pages to be budgeted for the magazine(s) under his or her direction as does the publisher in a decentralized system. He or she will ask the members of the sales force to study and advise as to the number of advertising pages each salesperson expects to sell for the calendar or fiscal year ahead. Similar forms used by publishers in decentralized systems will be used here. The publisher will then review the submissions of his or her sales staff and, based on experience, will determine the precise number of pages to be included in the budget for each magazine.

Under the centralized system of operation, the profitability will be determined by a management committee consisting of the chairman, the president, the editorial director, and the controller.

This management committee will set the necessary parameters for the publisher to follow, and only after receiving the required data from the publisher will the committee begin its work.

In addition to determining the number of pages of advertising to be scheduled for each magazine, the publisher develops a marketing and promotional program, including set goals for the year ahead.

Departmental Functions

Along with the editorial, production, and circulation departments, advertising is one of the four cornerstones of a specialized business magazine operation. It is the publisher, as overseer of advertising, who is more often than not the key to the success of a business magazine.

Though the position of publisher may differ somewhat with the company involved, his or her major responsibilities remain the same. For instance, at Magazines For Industry, Inc. (MFI) (now part of HBJ Publications, a division of Harcourt Brace Jovanovich, Inc.), the present group publisher, who heads one of five profit centers, is the manager of the periodicals under his jurisdiction. By maintaining the highest level of excellence in each and thereby generating maximum income from subscriptions and advertising, the periodicals will show the highest possible contribution to overhead.

The following description of the workings of a business magazine advertising and sales department was contributed by one of MFI's publishers.

For a publisher to perform efficiently, he or she needs an effective staff, which typically includes an advertising sales manager, advertising sales personnel (the number depends on the size of the market and the magazine's potential), and an advertising secretary/coordinator, in addition to one or more secretaries and clerks. Specific duties of each are outlined below.

PUBLISHER

The publisher, as manager of periodicals, must have experience or knowledge of the workings of all departments. Not uncommonly a publisher has previously served as advertising manager or, in some cases, editor of a magazine.

In the advertising area, the publisher must not only plan advertising strategy to attract new advertisers but must anticipate and satisfy present customer's needs, while constantly monitoring costs.

In the editorial area, the publisher must determine the current and future needs of the magazine's audience and work with the editor and advertising manager (the publisher's "two right hands") to translate these needs into editorial content and advertising sales. When properly coordinated, the editor and advertising sales manager assist the publisher as finely tuned partners.

Specialized business magazine publishers must be experts in their marketplaces—to the point where they could be called upon to "save the day" if necessary in an advertising situation. In other words, a publisher should be able to make an effective advertising presentation.

The publisher can, furthermore, create a positive image for the publications and thereby for the entire advertising sales department by: writing a regular column in his or her magazine(s), speaking and/or participating at industry-related events, and/or seizing various opportunities to act as a spokesperson for the magazine(s) and the industry(ies) represented.

The publisher must also be an energizer, motivator, and coordinator of the sales personnel.

ADVERTISING SALES MANAGER

The advertising sales manager is chief of the advertising department staff. He or she is often considered a publisher-in-training (or a backup). The advertising sales manager is responsible for all aspects of managing the advertising department, including: (1) maintaining current advertising, (2) increasing volume of advertising from current advertisers, and (3) attracting future advertisers.

The advertising sales manager is also responsible for the development and maintenance of:

- Basic advertising records
- Records on the competition

- A media fact file
- Sales promotional literature
- Magazine advertising campaign
- Lists and samples of prospective advertisers
- Liaison with sales personnel
- Information channels to the publisher and the editor

Basic advertising records. These include correct data on contracts (which constitute a general commitment to run advertising) and insertion orders (specific commitments, including issue date, specific advertisement, size, and color of ad, as well as code numbers where appropriate.)

In this regard, the advertising sales manager must also direct the preparation of a periodic advertising schedule (indicating what ads will run in which issues and which special ad positions are involved) for the production department. In the makeup of the issue, the advertising sales manager strives to ensure that competitive ads are not placed opposite each other and to maintain a positive competitive balance insofar as placing ads in front-of-the-book and right-hand positions. A high regard for details—prices, names, addresses, dates—is critical.

Records on the competition. All ads appearing in competitive magazines must be recorded as soon as they appear, with an indication of their size, color, and date of appearance. These records help identify where the business is—what percentage of advertising the sales manager's magazine is carrying, and the potential of the marketplace. For this information to be of maximum value, the advertising sales manager must communicate it to advertising salespersons.

A media fact file. A media fact file is similar to an aritist's portfolio and contains (generally in an attractively designed folder) current data on the magazine, including: statement of editorial purpose, editorial outline, examination of competitive editorial products, closing dates, circulation audit results, competitive circulation data, the advertising rate card, an examination of competitive advertising positions, and various announcements of special services. The media fact file must be updated continuously. Some publishing companies prepare data from their media files in slide form or for flip-chart presentation. In addition, many media fact files include a media comparability form—called an MCC form—that allows comparison of publications. Secondary audits and specialized readership studies may also be included.

Sales promotion literature. As budgets permit and the need arises (items often in conflict), the advertising sales manager will direct the preparation of special sales promotion literature. This material will often focus on a special journal issue or newly developed competitive edge.

Magazine advertising campaign. Specialized business magazines often run self-promotional advertisements in specialized publications such as *Standard Rate & Data Service, Advertising Age,* and *Industrial Marketing.* The advertising sales manager often creates and directs campaigns of this type.

Lists and samples of prospective advertisers. The advertising sales manager clips ads from competitive and related publications to pass along to sales personnel for their follow-up. Simultaneously, the advertising sales manager updates lists of names and addresses of key prospects and their advertising agency personnel (in order to keep them informed about the magazine). The advertising sales manager also commonly mails to these persons sample copies of his or her company's other magazines.

Liaison with all sales personnel. This is accomplished via call reports— brief periodic synopses of key developments in each account that salespersons prepare for the advertising sales manager. By examining these reports, the advertising sales manager can detect trends, coordinate seemingly unconnected data, and detect potential problem areas. By communicating such information to the salespersons, the advertising manager acts as an information clearinghouse.

Information channels to the publisher and the editor. In periodic discussions with the publisher and editor, the advertising sales manager conveys information relating, for example, to potential industry trends or potential stories. Such reports often come from advertising sales staff. (Note: One way that an effective editorial staff stays on top of new developments is to take advantage of leads from traveling advertising sales personnel. Conversely, an effective advertising sales staff can profit greatly from advertising prospects passed along by editorial personnel.)

ADVERTISING SPACE SALES PERSONNEL

An advertising space salesperson travels periodically throughout a given territory, soliciting advertising and maintaining relationships. An effective salesperson understands that service is a key part of developing these interpersonal relationships. To accomplish this he or she has several available tools: personal visits, telephone visits, and correspondence.

Personal visits. These should be choreographed as carefully as a ballet. Many checkpoints exist, among them:

- Who should be called on at the account?
- Who should be called on at the agency?
- When should these calls be made?
- Who carries which specific title?
- Who carries which specific responsibility?
- Who is rising in importance in the company?
- Who is losing ground?
- What materials to bring?
- What materials to leave?
- When to extend an invitation to lunch?
- When to extend an invitation to dinner?
- How close should a relationship become?
- Where should a meeting take place?

Telephone calls. Telephone calls are a separate art form. Among matters worth consideration are correct titles, correct appellations, appropriate time of day, length of call, and tone of conversation.

Correspondence. An often overlooked but key sales device is correspondence. Sometimes, for example, it is more effective not to leave a particular document during a personal visit but to include it in a follow-up letter. Not only what is written, but its length and the manner in which it is displayed can be vital.

In evaluating his or her use of these sales tools, a salesperson should constantly ask:

- Have I established my magazine's identity?
- Have I established my identity?
- How can I save my customer's time?

ADVERTISING SECRETARY/COORDINATOR

An efficient secretary enables the advertising sales personnel and advertising sales manager to save time and to perform efficiently. This reflects well on the whole publishing operation.

Editorial Department

Editorial copy preparation has three distinct phases: manuscript preparation, composition, and makeup.

MANUSCRIPT PREPARATION

Manuscript preparation and production for a specialized business periodical differs from that for a book publishing and/or magazine publishing company, depending on the size of the operation and the type of composition and printing used. What follows is an example of the manner in which production work is done by one magazine of a medium-sized publishing organization. In some ways, it is typical. However, a large operation such as the business magazine group of Harcourt Brace Jovanovich follows a more sophisticated—that is, more automated—procedure. Various facets of the overall editorial process for specialized business periodicals have already been touched on in former chapters (and are covered in depth in other books—see Bibliography in the appendixes). This discussion focuses on some mechanical aspects of manuscript preparation, using *Food & Drug Packaging*, a Magazines For Industry, Inc., publication as an example.

Editors are given specifications for typing their copy (number of characters per line of typeset copy) so that they can gauge the length of the printed piece in the magazine. Typed copy is always double-spaced.

On the upper left-hand corner of each manuscript page the copy is slugged (or identified) as to subject matter, specific issue date for which it has been written, and the typesetting specifications (specs). (On occasion, the individual editor's identification might also be included, thus facilitating subsequent inquiries by those doing the copy editing.)

Copy is proofread using standard proofreader's marks (see Webster's New Collegiate Dictionary).

The source material—that is the reporter's notes, press release data, and other information—is stapled to a carbon copy of the story as a reference for the copy editor. Three editors edit the copy, checking for language flow, accuracy, and any questions that the copy leaves unanswered. (In this latter respect, the editor acts as a surrogate business periodical reader.)

Once edited and initialed by the three editors, copy is sent to the typesetter, who follows the specifications provided to set the type, producing photoreproducible galley proofs (called "repro" proofs). Photocopies of these repro proofs are then sent to the editors, who proofread the galleys against the submitted manuscript and return the corrected galleys to the typesetter.

COMPOSITION

The second phase of editorial production is composition. At Magazines For Industry, phototypesetting is performed in-house. Two systems are employed: First, a phototypesetter for body type (offering type sizes from 6 to 36 points), captions, and selected headings, plus a photoprocessor. This equipment requires a trained operator and generates justified and hyphenated copy in column format ready for paste-up. Second, for news style heads and other off-line copy in the 14 to 72 point range, a typesetter called a "headliner" and a smaller photoprocessor are required. This system does not require a trained operator. Editors can operate the headliner with minimal (less than one-half hour) training. The headliner has a standard typewriter keyboard with about a dozen or so special-function keys to enable the editor to select one of the two typefaces that its drum accommodates. A library of typeface film strips are available for mounting on the drum. The desired type size is dialed, the headline typed out, and the photosensitive paper on which the copy is placed is put into the photoprocessor. In seconds, the headline type emerges from the processor.

MAKEUP

The third and final stage of editorial production is the makeup phase in which pages of the magazine are designed and pasted up.

To aid in planning both feature and news layouts, the production department, after consultation with the editors, provides editors with a "thumbnail" or imposition guide to the issue. This gives the editor an indication of the overall number of editorial pages versus number of ads, the location of color pages, and the location of editorial and ad copy in the book. The imposition sheet is the central document for building a specific issue.

On *Food & Drug Packaging*, the makeup phase is handled in two different ways: Feature material is gathered by the editorial staff and given to the art department for page design, and news pages are designed by the editorial staff.

For feature pages, the editor first determines how much space the feature is likely to need and communicates this to the production director. Galleys are collected; the headline and subheads, as well as any captions, are written; and this material, plus the repro proofs, are sent to the art department along with an editorial production form which gives instructions on space to be left for photographs and use of color. Using the repro proofs, the art department pastes up a camera-ready version of each page, called a "mechanical," which, after being checked by the editorial department, is sent to the printer.

News pages are handled slightly differently in that the "inverted pyramid" philosophy is carried out in the design of the pages. Here the editorial staff, using a stripped (cut up) photocopy of the repros, pastes down the pages as they would like to see them appear, sets specific headlines on the headliner, and pastes photocopies of these in place before giving the finished rough layouts to the art department for production of a "mechanical."

Once the news and feature pages are in mechanical form, the art department makes a photocopy of the entire page and gives this "page proof" to the editorial staff to check for corrections. Once approved, the mechanicals are sent to the printer, who produces a set of "blues" or early proofs of the issue in signature form. These blues give the editorial, art, and production staffs a final chance to check their respective contributions and verify that the printer has not made any changes in the material. When the blues are approved, the printer uses them as an okay to print the publication.

Production Department

Once the editor and his or her staff have written and edited the contents of an issue, and the publisher and sales manager have finished scheduling that issue's advertising, the production staff takes over the final function of producing the magazine and making it ready for the printer, binder, and mailer. Following is a description of the organization and functions of a production department (Magazines for Industry, Inc., now part of HBJ Publications) that handles nine medium-size periodicals and nine other publishing properties that include biannuals, annuals, newsletters, and a technical book division. In 1981, it installed an in- house electronic typesetting system for all of its periodicals.

STAFF AND RESPONSIBILITIES

The production department has a staff of four: a production director, two production managers, and one production assistant. Their responsibilities are as follows:

Production director. The production director of this company heads the department and is also directly involved with two magazines—that is, doing the trafficking (processing of advertising contracts and insertion orders), making the impositions, and coordinating with the printer and editorial staff. He or she also buys paper as well as printing services and handles special projects for the company.

Production managers. Each production manager is responsible for three magazines, as well as for any related directories, catalogs, or manuals. The managers compile all information and material pertinent to the makeup of the current issues. They relay necessary information and material (such as art, photographs, and advertisements to be shot for an issue) to the printer and make necessary changes. They coordinate with and help the printer, publisher, editorial, and production staffs to keep on schedule.

Production assistant. He or she assists the production director, mainly in trafficking of ads, and does some impositions where necessary.

PRODUCTION OPERATIONS

Insertion orders. Copies of each insertion order are sent to the production department from the advertising department on an issue-to- issue basis. Each insertion order is processed, and information pertinent to the makeup of the magazine—such as size, shape, color, position in the issue, ad caption for identification, status of material, and necessary corrections—is entered on the advertising schedule. This information is then referred to in the makeup of the issue, in checking page proofs and blue lines to make sure ads are run correctly, and in billing.

Trafficking of ads. Before makeup, the ads are trafficked. That is, if proper information is not included on an insertion order, the production manager contacts the agency or advertiser to verify what ad material will be run. Trafficking becomes necessary only when there are no instructions, when material is late in coming, or when instructions conflict. When calls are made, deadlines are stressed, and extensions granted when possible. When material comes in, it is checked and recorded on an ad schedule sheet, and the material is sent to the printer with an order form and explicit printing instructions. The printer is also told which ads to pick up (repeat) from previous issues (tear sheets of ads from the previous issue which are to be picked up are included).

Makeup. At makeup time the production manager receives editorial requirements from the editor and special instructions regarding ads from the publisher. The production manager and publisher determine the size of the book (as earlier noted, "book" is a printer's term for any periodical), always endeavoring to keep a good editorial/ad ratio. Impositions are prepared carefully, with attention paid to printer's specifications for the most economical press layout. From these impositions, a thumbnail (a chart denoting page-by-page placement of advertising) is prepared. This is given to the publisher, who checks to be sure that competitive ads are not on facing pages, and makes sure that all scheduled ads will appear in the issue.

The editor then receives a copy of the thumbnail and plans editorial content around the advertising. The production manager pastes ads into position on dummy pages, then gives them to the editorial department to dummy editorial material around the ads.

Coordination with printer. By this time, the issue is close to its final form, with no major changes expected. At this point, the production manager gives detailed written instructions to the printer including:

1. General breakdown of forms, type of imposition, and how to run signatures
2. Paper to be used for each signature
3. Description of inserts and binding instructions for each
4. Impositions for each form/signature indicating page, color, size, and shape

Dummy pages are sent to the printer, who processes and returns them and a set of page proofs to the production department. (Note: In this particular company's operation, the printer prepares the pasted up mechanical. In other operations, a company's art department or perhaps an outside typesetter or graphic arts firm would handle this.) The production manager checks and makes corrections on all page proofs that have ads on them. The editorial staff checks all editorial copy. Page proofs are then returned to the printer, who makes corrections and returns a final proof (blue lines) to production for a last check.

Wrap-up. After each issue, the production manager checks all printing bills against contracts, making sure that instructions were followed and charges are correct. Rebilling forms for work done on ads are filled out and sent to the accounting department along with printing bills.

Production papers, insertion orders, and ad proofs are filed.

Circulation and Distribution Department

Although rapidly changing technology, among other things, has made circulation a highly complex function, its basic goals have not changed since the inception of periodical publishing. Circulation is no longer simply reader development and maintenance, however, but an integral part of business periodical marketing and publishing, incorporating sophisticated computer programs to meet specific marketing needs.

STAFF AND RESPONSIBILITIES

Today's circulation director must have diverse knowledge ranging from accounting to promotion; he or she must be an administrator of budgets and personnel and, in addition, must understand the application of computer technology and programming to circulation goals. While a circulation director is basic to a successful business periodical, the extent of his or her staff varies. Publishers operating with their own circulation departments handle mailings that involve masses of paperwork and data that must be carefully filed for quick retrieval. Most circulation departments must buy at least a portion of the fulfillment operation, since owning a computer or even buying time on one can be prohibitively expensive. This decision depends on the number and size of periodicals involved and, of course, on the number of subscribers and potential recipients.

Fulfillment companies put the smallest publishers in the same league as major companies. By using such services, publishers can keep personnel numbers down, can control costs, and, even more importantly, can retain control over their lists.

One efficient circulation department clerk can generally handle 20,000 names on a controlled (free) circulation magazine. On paid publications, the preferred number of names per clerk is smaller—one clerk per 10,000 names. This is because paid publications are almost always more complicated, requiring, in addition to regular coding and filing procedures, a caging operation (money handling) and renewal records. Circulation department clerks translate reader responses into publisher mailings, or telephone contacts into code numbers with names and addresses for storage in the fulfillment service's computer.

The fulfillment service can provide circulation counts for print orders; a variety of demographic breakouts (by title, geographic location, etc.); and labels for publication mailing.

Publishers can operate without a circulation department by employing any of a number of available professional services. These replace all the functions of a circulation department except management; they do the mailings, keep records, handle cash receipts, etc. One drawback is that the fees for such work are subject to annual, and usually substantial, increases. This is largely because once a publisher becomes committed to this type of circulation maintenance, it is extremely difficult to change companies, let alone set up or return to an internal department. A major reason for this is time. Keeping a circulation list up-to-date, for example, requires: mailings (with reply cards) or telephone contacts to current recipients to verify their interest; contacts with potential new readers to replace those who have failed to respond; and contacts to renew paid subscribers and obtain new ones. All of this communication produces documents to be processed or records to be changed (for the audit) in order to keep a list from aging.

EFFECTIVE CIRCULATION MANAGEMENT

Preventing circulation deterioration is a daily challenge. A controlled circulation list containing names last verified three years past lessens the publisher's credibility and reduces reader responsiveness, ultimately damaging a publication's marketability.

A good circulation list is never static, even for a day. As people change jobs within companies or move to others, their replacements must be incorporated onto a periodical's circulation list to keep it current. The more rapidly these changes are entered, the better the publication serves its readers and benefits advertisers.

Audits. By keeping a circulation list current and properly documented, the requirements of the major audit bureaus are met, as well. As mentioned earlier in this chapter, the two most widely recognized audit bureaus are BPA (Business Publications Audit) and ABC (Audit Bureau of Circulations). Both are independent of publishers, but supported by them. In checking the validity of a publication's circulation, an audit agency functions somewhat like an accounting firm conducting a financial audit; it sends auditors to examine the publisher's records relating to printing, geographic distribution, post-office receipts, and indications of reader receipt of and desire for the publication.

Audits are conducted once a year, with publisher's unaudited statements issued alternately to cover a six-month period. Both are printed forms distributed to advertising agencies, advertising companies, and publishers. The reports include information such as: qualified-reader circulation distribution numbers by issue, average distribution, geographic distribution, qualified-reader title breakout, and other industry information (e.g., plant volume related to readership). *Qualified* is the key word: Publishers must define the market served and the types of executives sought as recipients; these become "qualified" readers.

Sources and procedures used to validate "qualified" readers are as follows:

- Personal written request from a recipient—most often a reply card resulting from a publisher's mailing
- Written request from recipient's firm—a document from an executive designating others in his or her company to whom the publication is to be sent
- Written communication from recipient or firm other than request—a document offering names of others in the industry who should receive the publication
- Association rosters and directories
- Business directories
- Independent field report—for example a Dun & Bradstreet Corportation listing, or data from Harvey Research Organization
- Licenses (federal, state, and local)—names taken from such documents issued by government agencies
- Manufacturer, distributor, and wholesaler lists—sales prospects of those supplying goods and services to potential readers
- Telephone interviews

Should claims made by a publisher fail to be substantiated, the audit agencies point this out in the forms mentioned earlier. In cases where the publisher has incomplete records or where fraudulent documentation is discovered, the publication is suspended from membership in the audit agency (until records are made valid), and notices are sent to advertising agencies, advertisers, and competing publishers, all of whom react strongly to such reports. On rare occasions publishers are divested entirely of their membership, but this occurs only when fraud is proved and management is involved.

Retaining and acquiring readers. To maintain and improve circulation, a variety of sources are employed to obtain lists of potential qualified readers, both for controlled and paid publications. These include the most up-to-date directories, association membership rolls, trade show attendance lists, employee lists of companies in the market, customer lists of suppliers to the market, government agencies at all levels, and so forth.

These names are solicited most often by direct mail, and sometimes by telephone. Mailings are usually composed of a letter and a postage-paid return form, containing specific questions regarding the recipient's function and his or her firm's business. The key question on the form is always, "Do you wish to receive this publication—Yes or No?" A signature and date on the document are also vital to its validity. In general, questions on the forms are designed to gain information which is important to advertisers in identifying market potential or in determining a publication's ability to exploit this potential. Certain questions are often required because of a comparability program introduced by BPA.

The comparability program, designed to make the review of competitive publications simpler for prospective advertisers, arranges for publishers serving the same market to agree on a set of basic questions that all will ask of readers. Responses are reported on circulation statements and are subject to audit by BPA. Those publishers unwilling to agree on comparability, some for practical reasons, may be placed in a category indicating that they have not cooperated in this respect.

Telephone solicitations ask similar questions as do written mailings, but are more direct and achieve considerably faster responses. They are also vastly more expensive, which makes a difference on controlled publications, but is simply another cost of producing income on paid magazines. Telephone contacts are generally followed by mailings, particularly on paid publications.

To keep a circulation list current, recipients must be contacted often enough to keep them in the one-year verified category. To do this, one-twelfth of the recipients are contacted (by mail mostly) each month. Recipients contacted are those whose paid or request forms will expire shortly in the one-year category. By this procedure, most of the circulation is kept in the one-year category (considered totally valid), while those moving into the two-year category (still broadly acceptable) can still be pursued. Some publishers retain readers into the third year, but this category has become questionable in our mobile society.

To replace "lost" names, the publisher returns to the list sources mentioned earlier. If time does not permit contacting potential recipients to obtain direct verification, the names can be added to circulation by qualifying through directories and other sources.

Adding names at any time, but particularly when selecting from list sources, creates a potentially serious problem of duplication—as when two different lists contain the same name, but entered differently enough that the computer accepts both. Names added must be carefully checked against current circulation lists to avoid sending duplicate copies of the publication, possibly leading to an inflated circulation figure that auditors will question.

Promotion by direct mail is the most popular means of keeping old and obtaining new paid subscribers. Such promotions range from elaborate four-color mailings offering premiums (subscription inducements—such as a book with a dollar value of half or less than the subscription value) to simple promotional letters, both most often with reply envelopes so that payment can come with the order. When orders are returned with "Bill Me" requests, these are entered as credit subscriptions, acceptable to the audit agency if payment is made within three months. Follow-up on these subscriptions is expensive, but vital, as is all promotion on paid circulation publications.

The cost of obtaining a paid subscription is often equal to the income; sometimes it is more expensive. Some publishers continue to regard paid subscription circulation as more valid than controlled, unless the latter is all one-year direct request.

Paid circulation publications expend much effort to retain readers, far more than do controlled publications, since renewal percentages are used to measure how well subscribers regard the product. To achieve acceptable or better renewal rates (approximately 60 percent renewal is considered acceptable; over 70 percent is good; above 80 percent is excellent), publishers employ several devices. Most prevalent is a series of mailings, the average number being five, starting two months before and continuing three months after expiration of a subscription.

In addition to mailings, telephone services are employed to follow up directly with "expired" subscriptions. These services are generally used by the publisher as a last resort, since telephone services retain as their fee 100 percent of the subscription payment or more, if the subscription is not high enough.

To achieve renewals of paid subscriptions or requalifications of controlled circulation requires careful attention to detail and voluminous records. Such records also figure importantly in establishing proper print and distribution orders for each issue of a publication.

Print orders, labels, and other areas. Computer reports of current circulation provide the basis for establishing the print and distribution orders for each issue (how many copies the printer is to print, and where and how they are to be distributed—United States, foreign; land, sea, or airmail). Since circulation lists are constantly active, print orders can change for each issue. Most publishers, however, update lists once a month, even if publication frequency is weekly or fortnightly. On paid circulation publications this can lead to complaints, for it can take as much as eight weeks for a new name to be processed. For this reason, publishers sometimes fulfill new orders with labels separately prepared in-house.

When labels are provided for mailing, they must meet certain post office requirements, such as zip code sequence. Each issue mailed also requires submission of certain post office forms.

Establishing a mailing privilege and entry point (post office from which the issue is mailed) is another function of the circulation department. (Establishing the entry point is a matter of meeting postage class requirements for the publication and submitting the proper forms.)

Besides providing for mailing of a publication, circulation departments are often involved in direct mail marketing of circulation lists to other companies, associations, trade show managers, etc., who wish to promote a product or service. This often results in substantial revenue for the publisher. The more finely a list can be broken down according to type of product, geography, title of recipient, plant size, etc., the more marketable it becomes.

Labels produced for such mailings are rarely provided directly to the purchaser, but are handled through a reputable mailing house. The reason for this is simple and basic to publishing—a publication's circulation list is its very being and must be cared for and protected.

Because of the complexities involved in circulation and the special technical terminology used, a special training program for circulation personnel may be needed and may prove highly valuable. Therefore, the appendixes to this book contain a Training Program for Circulation Personnel, developed with the help of one of the major fulfillment companies serving the magazine field. The program should help to inform circulation personnel about the specialized aspects of their job.

CHAPTER 7

The Leadership Function

Though the basic purpose of a specialized business periodical is to provide its readers with news and information, there is another, equally important role for some business periodical publishers and editors. This is leadership.

Specialized business periodicals that are engaged in leadership activities have been able to help shape the direction of the industries they serve; some have actually played a vital role in creating new industries and/or altering industries to the point where these become new fields of business. Business magazines have been involved, for example, in sponsoring and conducting seminars on industry problems, in developing and managing trade shows, in setting up award programs, and in helping to further (or in actually forming) technical and scientific societies or associations. The benefits to publications participating in such activities have been both improved financial status and heightened prestige.

This chapter contains several case histories to demonstrate the value and effectiveness of the leadership function exercised by today's specialized business periodical.

Creating a New Business

Until the mid-1950s, the kitchen business was not a discrete industry, but rather was part of the overall furniture and utensil field and included a variety of dealers and contractors. Complete built-in kitchens were sold by appliance dealers, lumber yards, home improvement dealers, and other companies. Following is the story of how kitchen products became an industry unto itself, with specialized retailers and distributors who continue to enjoy a spectacular record of growth.

Lawrence and Milton Gralla, business periodical journalists with an entrepreneurial bent, formed a business news bureau in 1951 to serve the specialized business press in the same way that the Associated Press and other news services serve newspapers. Within a few years, the Gralla operation served hundreds of specialized business periodicals covering diverse fields. As time went on, the Gralla brothers noted that although they were obtaining a great deal of news about kitchen-related products, there was no specialized magazine covering what seemed to be a growing and exciting business area. They decided to launch one themselves. Thus, in September 1955, they introduced a monthly, coated-paper tabloid and called it simply *Kitchen Business*, while also continuing their business news service, "just in case . . . ."

Two things happened. First, within a short time, the publication, *Kitchen Business*, led to the creation of a totally separate kitchen industry. It did this by providing vital information to dealers and distributors, discussing production methods and supply sources for manufacturers, and helping makers of appliances, cabinets, hardware, and accessories to define the market. It also supported and stimulated the start of kitchen schools, and originated a national kitchen industry convention as well as related business programs of the dealer groups participating in such programs. The second development was that *Kitchen Business*, through its content and advertising, helped to accelerate the growth of kitchen product distributors—from the kitchen to the bath—and a variety of other industry building developments.

Kitchen Business also helped in the formation of the National Institute of Wood Kitchen Cabinets, established in 1955, and formulated and published, as well, the first built-in range and oven specifications in 1959. In succeeding years its founders and staff developed an annual kitchen industry exposition (including a series of seminars) that has become one of the largest trade shows of its kind.

As a result of their success with *Kitchen Business*, the Grallas started and acquired other specialized business magazines, with the result that by 1982 Gralla Publications had become one of the largest independent business magazine publishing companies in the United States, with annual advertising revenue exceeding $40 million.

Changing an Industry's Direction

A classic example of leadership in business magazine journalism is found in the history of *Home Center Magazine*, published by Vance Publishing Company of Chicago. The company was founded by Herbert Vance in 1937 with one magazine. Today Vance publishes more than 20 periodicals, runs a trade show, operates a video production division, and serves a broad range of industries and professions in other ways.

Home Center Magazine, of which George L. Milne, a veteran publishing executive, is publishing director, started life as *American Lumberman* in 1873. It owes its continuing vitality to the fact that it has continually proved its ability to change direction with the industry it serves, while anticipating new trends. Today, the magazine is credited with helping to create the home center branch of the home remodeling industry.

In 1960, observing the transition of the conventional lumber dealer (serving principally builders) to a retailer of home remodeling, maintenance, decorating, and repair products, *American Lumberman* changed its name to *Building Material Merchandiser*. It kept this title until 1972, at which time the publisher realized that the industry's direction was changing once again.

At that time, a variety of publications were commenting about the development of a new concept—the home center market. These included hardware, discount, and building materials dealer periodicals. But no one was serving this emerging field exclusively. Accordingly, in 1972, Milne recommended to the Vance management that the magazine's name be changed to *Home Center Magazine*, and that its editorial content be redirected to serve this field exclusively. In addition, Milne proposed the establishment of a strict, well-defined qualification standard for those who would be invited to receive the magazine, and also that the company's marketing and research efforts should be focused on furthering the growth of the home center industry.

Vance endeavored to do all these things but, unfortunately, the recession of 1973 to 1975 retarded the growth of the periodical just as it did the industry. As a result, the magazine ended the year in 1975 with only 277 pages of advertising and an editorial content that did not meet the original expectations.

Nevertheless, the magazine, with the full backing of the publishing company, persevered, and soon launched a number of creative projects that eventually accomplished its original goals and at the same time helped to develop the home center industry into a stable and growing field. In 1979, the magazine published over 800 paid advertising pages, with an equal number of high-quality editorial pages. Following are the principal steps that *Home Center Magazine* took to reach its objectives:

- It adopted editorial content designed to show retailers how to carry out useful, innovative, and successful ideas to attract and serve the do-it-yourself consumer—today's fastest growing user of products for home improvement, remodeling, decorating, and maintenance.
- It developed a continuous program of industry research that has established the magazine as a major authority in home center retailing.
- It initiated a biannual *Profile of Home Centers,* one of a group of major studies conducted by *Home Center Magazine.*
- It established, sponsored, and managed the National Home Center/Home Improvement Congress and Exposition. This was one of the most successful new trade shows to have been introduced in this country in the 1970s. In four years it grew from 600 exhibiting companies to more than 1,200, and industry attendance jumped from 12,000 the first year to over 21,000 in 1979. The program includes educational seminars and the International Home Center Marketing Conference.

Helping to Save an Industry

Business magazines have also been instrumental in rescuing smaller industries through encouraging merger with larger ones. An example is provided by *Modern Tire Dealer*, a publication of Bill Communications, Inc., New York.

Modern Tire Dealer is not published in New York but in Akron, Ohio, in the heart of the tire business. For years, *Modern Tire Dealer* has been a leading force in helping and educating the independent tire dealer. But it went a bit further. By means of a well-organized campaign, the magazine was successful in putting the independent tire dealer in the automotive service business, a step that did much to ensure the future of independent tire dealers.

Shortly after 1960, *Modern Tire Dealer* established the editorial position that tire dealers should diversify—should go beyond selling and installing tires exclusively—if they were to remain viable and profitable. As a result of the magazine's consistent and hard-hitting editorial program, and despite the fact that longer-wearing radial tires are in vogue, dealers have become full automotive merchandisers, selling and installing a variety of products. Without this expansion, tire dealers would have had a difficult time staying in business.

Modern Tire Dealer included specific recommendations for its readers, showing them how they could expand into the total automotive merchandising field by offering wheel alignment, brake service, shocks, tune-ups, and mufflers, in addition to tire sales. It also educated dealers in the business aspects of such expansion, such as investment required, needed space and equipment, personnel, service intervals, costs systems, pricing, and profit potentials. The magazine's readers took the advice and information to heart and proceeded to expand successfully.

Defining an Industry's Market

Plastics Technology, a standard-size monthly also published by Bill Communications, has remained an active force in the plastics industry by helping to define, document, and quantify the industry's market, thus establishing a clear line between the plastics industry and its markets.

Beginning in the late 1940s and continuing today, more and more of the so-called "end-using" industries of plastics have, as the volume of plastics consumption increased, manufactured their own plastic components. Early in the 1960s, *Plastics Technology* determined to define as its readership marketplace those involved in the processing or manufacturing of plastics. More specifically, it defined its readers as those employed at any plant owning and operating plastics-processing equipment, regardless of whether the plant was a custom processor or was an end-user, such as the automotive industry, communications field, or appliance business. The magazine developed a computerized list—a kind of census—of the industry, including all of those plants and individuals involved in the processing of plastics. The census has been ongoing, so that today the magazine, and its advertisers, continue to be able to gauge and define the growing and changing plastics industry.

Developing Trade Organizations

Several periodicals have assumed key roles in the formation of professional societies, industry associations, and technical groups, especially in the highly specialized, emerging technical fields. Here are a few examples:

Materials Handling Engineering, a Penton/IPC magazine, was instrumental in founding the Materials Handling Institute, while the company's *Hydraulics* and *Pneumatics* periodicals played a similar role in the development of the National Fluid Power Association and later, the Fluid Power Society.

In 1946, *Candy Industry* (now of HBJ Publications, Inc.), then in its second full year of operation, founded, with a number of industry leaders, the American Association of Candy Technologists (AACT), today a large (with membership over 600) and important scientific and technical society that has been instrumental in the initiation and fostering of major technical developments of confectionery manufacturing.

The AACT now holds an annual convention jointly with that of the National Confectioners Association, the manufacturers' group, and also holds (through sections and regional societies) periodic area meetings in various parts of the country at which scientific papers in the technical developments area are presented. The AACT has been a vital force in encouraging sound product development, quality control, and the use of new ingredients, in addition to raising the standards of the manufacturing phase of the industry.

Sponsoring Industry Awards

In 1945, *Candy Industry* established the Kettle Award, which each year presents a replica of a copper kettle (symbolic of the confectionery manufacturing industry) to the Candy Industry Man, or Woman, who during the prior year performed distinguished service on behalf of the industry. The Kettle Award has been recognized as the "Oscar" of the confectionery industry and its presentation has become the star attraction of the National Confectioners Association's annual convention.

The monthly periodical *Beverage Industry* also has an annual award, presented to chief executives and chief operating officers of soft drink bottling companies, breweries, and bottled water, juice, or wine plants, who have outstanding records of industry achievement.

Glass Industry similarly offers an annual achievement award, called the Phoenix Trophy, as do a number of other publications.

Awards of this type have generated substantial interest on the part of executives to serve their industries in extraordinary ways. Thus, leadership on the part of periodicals has generated leadership in the industries they serve, the end result being improved technology, marketing, and management approaches, and better products for the consumer.

PART III

Areas of Growth Potential

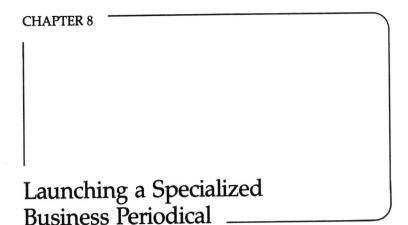

CHAPTER 8

Launching a Specialized Business Periodical

One of the most exciting projects an entrepreneur can undertake is to launch a new specialized business periodical. While the risks are substantial, so are the rewards. The risks involve investments—in dollars, time, and energy. But if the periodical proves successful, the rewards can be both personally and financially fulfilling.

The investment needed to start a specialized business periodical is today considerably higher than it was several decades ago, but it remains much smaller than that required to promote and publish a large-circulation consumer magazine.

What kind of person or group launches a new specialized business periodical? Typically, the person is either an editor or an editorially oriented publishing executive of an existing company who has been unable to sell an idea for a new magazine to management—or an individual who simply wishes to go out on his or her own with a creative idea for a new periodical.

Determining the Need

What are the essential prerequisites for success? First and foremost is the determination that a need exists (or can be quickly created) for the kind of periodical being considered. Unless a proven need exists (or is unmistakably on the horizon), the new publication is doomed. For example, a periodical may be needed

139

to provide important information currently unavailable through any other source; or to cover an emerging field of interest; or to replace existing industry publications that, in the entrepreneur's estimation, do not adequately serve the industry.

A good example of an independently started magazine designed to cover an aspect of industry neglected by other periodicals is *Pharmaceutical Technology*. Its founder and publisher had been a successful space salesperson for an eastern publisher. He was in his mid-twenties, self-taught, creative, and anxious to "run his own show."

His idea for a new publication was based on the fact that while a few existing magazines covered the marketing and business interests of the pharmaceutical industry, none dealt with its technical aspects. After spending two months doing preliminary market research and verifying the need for such a periodical, he made the commitment (in November 1976) to forge ahead with the new publishing venture.

"I knew that I would be dealing with the most quality-conscious industry," he explained, "and, as a consequence, the magazine had to reflect the same high level of quality." He therefore hired an editor with a strong background in magazine publishing. The two then proceeded to plan the new publication, deciding initially to concentrate on the editorial approach, content, and the selling of advertising, and later to establish plans for production, circulation, copy editing, and research. At the outset, the publisher sold all the advertising himself, did all the market planning, and developed promotional materials.

Volume 1, Number 1, of *Pharmaceutical Technology* was scheduled for June 1977, and was published on target. It appeared as a monthly instead of a bimonthly. (Bimonthly frequency is more commonly chosen by entrepreneurs; however, the publisher of *Pharmaceutical Technology* reasoned that the enormous information needs of the industry warranted a monthly right from the start.) The decision proved to be correct.

The magazine was successful from the beginning. The first issue contained 88 pages, 39 of which were advertising. By the end of the first year, a profitable future was virtually assured, and by 1979, advertising revenue reached $1 million.

By 1982, *Pharmaceutical Technology* had become widely

respected and read. Its success is founded, first of all, on the fact that it provides a forum for peer recognition as well as for an increased exchange of technical (and regulatory) information. The magazine established a policy of being neither pro-industry nor pro-government, but of encouraging the expression of all viewpoints. Winning the confidence and trust of both industry and government, and thus improving communication between the two, has been a strong point of the magazine. Interaction between reader and publisher has also received high priority, leading to timely editorial content. Finally, the advertising has presented technical information on products and equipment.

Establishing a Budget and a Prospectus

Once the need for a periodical is verified, the next step is to set up a budget and develop a prospectus, both of which can be used to obtain needed financing. Rarely does an entrepreneur have sufficient personal funds to launch a new publication. A good rule of thumb is that a beginning publisher should have enough funds to continue to publish for at least a full year without a profit; two or three years would obviously be better. In addition, it will take at least a year before it is known whether the new magazine will have a profitable future, and usually at least three years before it breaks even (five years is not uncommon).

Thus, it is important to determine the break-even point in terms of the number of needed advertising pages per issue. If the break-even point is more than 35 pages of advertising per issue, sufficient financing should be obtained to carry on without profit for at least three years. If the break-even point is 50 or more pages, the project should be abandoned unless the end rewards are almost assured and a substantial investment is available so that the publisher will be able to operate the magazine for at least five years without a profit.

In setting up a budget, the publisher should enlist the help of an accounting firm that has had some publishing experience. Prior to obtaining financing a prospectus must also be prepared that details the need, editorial scope, space-selling approaches to be used, basic activities of proposed departments in the magazine, and brief biographic information about key personnel. (While staffing must necessarily follow obtaining financing, the new publisher should at least plan ahead, determining hiring needs for the editorial, advertising sales, accounting, circulation, and production departments. Also, since costs for all departments must be included in the budget, budget preparation will necessitate consideration of staffing needs.)

The specific amount of initial capital required will depend on the scope of the market to be tapped; in other words, the magazine's projected circulation. Circulation cost elements to consider include printing, binding, and mailing (the costs of which are currently high and are bound to increase). While the publisher can control printing and binding costs to a degree, mailing charges are obviously beyond control.

Another important circulation cost involves use of a fulfillment company. The new publisher should obtain several bids before selecting a company.

Dealing with Venture Capitalists

Family members and investment-oriented friends are often desirable sources of capital. A commercial bank can also help to direct an entrepreneur to venture-capital sources, but commercial banks do not (normally) make loans for new periodicals. A U.S. Small Business Administration loan might also be investigated.

At this writing (1983), venture capitalists are again showing interest in helping to launch new companies. Their prime interest has traditionally been in taking an equity position in new high-technology companies. But a few venture capital companies will take a chance on a new specialized publication. Such companies expect to be rewarded generously for the risk capital they are investing. But the entrepreneurial publisher must make certain that he or she will control the company being formed. The equity given for such funds should represent a minority stockholding—no more than 20 percent, if possible, but no more than 33 1/3 percent under any circumstances. While 51 percent equity represents basic control, 66 2/3 percent is more desirable since under most state corporate law, it permits the publisher more leeway in operating the corporation—especially in such activities as issuing new stock and in mergers and acquisitions.

It is also important to include a buy-back arrangement as well as to provide terms for acquiring additional capital for expansion once the magazine is launched successfully. All such details and contingencies must be included in the contract. The assistance of an experienced attorney or accountant (or both) is essential. No matter what outside help is obtained, however, it is up to the publisher to know thoroughly what is included in the contract; he or she must not be afraid to ask questions.

It is important, also, to remember that no investor, including the venture capitalist, will invest in a business unless the principal stockholder, the entrepreneur, is also ready and willing to make some capital investment (usually 10 percent of the total investment). For example, if the initial financing required is $100,000, the entrepreneur must be prepared to provide a minimum investment of about $10,000. The investment is thought to "bind" the entrepreneur to the job ahead and give him or her greater impetus to succeed. If the would-be entrepreneur lacks sufficient "seed" money, he or she may be better off attempting to sell the idea to an existing publishing company in return for some minor equity and a long- term contract—or at least a long-term contract with a share of the profits of the proposed new magazine.

Not everyone with a practical idea for a new magazine is, in fact, qualified to become the owner or major stockholder of a business. It takes a strong desire to own a business, sufficient knowledge about operating a publishing company, and the ability to withstand the pressures that normally arise in beginning a new enterprise—not to mention the strength to abandon a well-paying position to strike out independently.

Undercapitalization has been the major reason for failure of beginning publishers. While some periodicals do show a profit within the first year of publication, this is the exception by far. As stated, it usually takes from three to five years to make a profit, and unless sufficient capital is available to "sweat it out" for so long a period, it may be best not to attempt the venture. In addition, no matter how carefully a budget is prepared, there are, inevitably, "unknowns."

Nevertheless, for those with the knowledge, persistence, and wherewithal, opportunities for new publications do exist. It is encouraging that even in an inflationary economy, the financial risk of launching a new business periodical with a fairly small circulation (no more than 25,000) can be reasonably small as compared to starting other types of business. And though the initial financial rewards of a profitable magazine may not be staggering, a publisher who succeeds with one business magazine can use the proceeds to launch others, and before long build up a sizable enterprise.

Timing in the Marketplace

A crucial problem for the successful one-publication publisher who is contemplating starting another involves timing—both in the marketplace and insofar as his other business is concerned. An expansion program must be well planned and structured, with additional publications started one at a time. Under no circumstances should a second periodical be attempted unless the first magazine is operating profitably and generating sufficient cash flow to support another publication. Such advice may seem elementary, but experience has shown that an entrepreneur who succeeds early with one magazine often begins to feel that starting a new business magazine is a "cinch." The result may be that a second venture is undertaken without proper planning and/or marketing research, and, worst of all, without the capital to continue publishing the new periodical for a longer period than it took to make the first one profitable.

Operating the New Periodical

Having secured the needed funds or a guaranteed commitment from a venture capitalist or other source, what are the entrepreneur's next steps? Following is a suggested schedule:

1. Determine the name of the magazine and decide on the format to be used.

2. Hire a staff as efficiently as possible. Be sure that the editor knows enough about the industry to be served (or at least can learn fast enough) to produce a thoroughly professional periodical. In the beginning, the editor should hire no more assistants than are absolutely necessary. The initial staff should also include a circulation manager or reliable outside circulation service, with the former preferred; a production manager, unless at least one of the editors to be hired is production oriented; and an accountant or outside accounting service (the former is definitely preferred).

3. Determine the kind (and amount) of circulation the magazine will need to efficiently cover its market, taking into account the circulation of competitive periodicals—and move diligently and quickly to develop the needed circulation program.

4. Hire a sales manager who knows the field and have him or her assemble an adequate number of capable and experienced space sales people.

5. Plan a promotional package—to include the initial rate card, the circulation "breakout" (which, within one year, will be ready for auditing by the BPA or ABC), and a start-up media fact file folder. In determining the contents of such folders (see also Chapter 6), it may help to obtain sample media file folders from successful magazines in unrelated fields.

6. Set up a timetable: date of first issue; editorial copy schedule; closing date for advertising material; and time of mailing. It may take six months to a year to put the first issue on press from the time the business is launched (i.e., from the point of staffing).

7. Set up a contractual arrangement with a printer, after meeting with several printers and obtaining at least three qualified bids.

8. Develop (and carefully review) the first year's budget, with special attention to the costs involved in producing the initial issue.

9. As to the organizational arrangement of individual departments, refer to earlier chapters in this book, particularly Chapters 5 and 6.

Why Some Succeed and Others Fail

Though there is no magic formula for ensuring the success of a business periodical, there are, in my experience, a few precepts worth following:

- Look for an industry that is just coming into its own, one that has no magazine or no particularly good one but has considerable potential for growth.
- Locate at least one sales-minded publisher and one competent editor, both with some experience or interest in the field.
- Strive to pick an industry that is fairly concentrated, so that circulation will be small or moderate—from 5,000 to 20,000 but in no case more than 50,000. And set up a rate structure that will provide sufficient income to produce a first-rate publication. For example, a periodical with a circulation of only 5,000 can demand an advertising rate of $1,700 per page, while a magazine with a circulation of 50,000 easily calls for a one-time page rate of $4,000 or higher. The only exception is in a fairly crowded field where one or more periodicals continue to publish with a lower rate than is warranted. (However, this type of publication is eventually doomed, for it will not be able to afford to produce a quality magazine and will thus lose its share of the market.)
- Be sure to organize properly. A strong, well-defined organization is vital.
- Run a "tight ship." It is amazing how much waste can be built into an operation. Be sure to budget effectively and to review budgets monthly. Make certain that the publisher or publishing executive in charge of each profit center (under the decentralized system of operation as outlined in Chapter 6) can account for each cost element.
- Though this is a labor-intensive business, additional personnel should not be added unless absolutely necessary. But make certain that existing staff represent the best talent available. Quality is more valuable than numbers.
- Operate on a decentralized basis, but make sure that the

magazine and/or magazines are carefully supervised by management.

Why do some business magazines or companies fail? Just as there is no easy formula for success, there is often no clear-cut reason for failure. However, there are some practices to avoid, particularly from an economic viewpoint. Here are a few of these:

- Poor planning, ineffective budgeting (or no budgeting at all), and failure on the part of management to supervise properly. Proper supervision means overseeing *every* department daily—from editorial to production to circulation—and, of course, fielding problems as they relate to the activities of the publishers.
- Failure to update or alter the periodical to conform to changing industry trends. It is essential not only to keep abreast of such movements but, better still, to anticipate them, and to maintain the flexibility necessary to make needed editorial and marketing changes swiftly.
- Failure to treat success cautiously. When a magazine succeeds beyond expectations (which does happen once in a while), there is a tendency to overspend. By the time management discovers the problems caused by extravagance, it may be too late. The same situation can be found in a fast-growing multi-publication company. Thus, it is imperative to examine all cost elements periodically and to require that publishers and department heads substantiate elements of increased cost.
- Failure to consider each new competitive magazine in the field a dangerous rival. New competition should not be disregarded, no matter how meager its beginnings. The new, insignificant magazine with an entrepreneurial tiger behind it may hungrily snatch an important share of the market of your magazine.
- Failure to bring new life into an organization. If one examines the failures of old-line magazines and companies that at one time published several successful periodicals, one dis-

covers that these operations did not infuse their periodicals and/or management staffs with new, young, and ambitious talent. Management that is set in its ways often spells the end of magazines and businesses. This is particularly true in the specialized business press, where creativity, ingenuity, and the ability to understand and accept changes in the marketplace are absolutely essential.

Much more could be written about launching a new specialized business periodical, but it is hoped that this discussion will prove a helpful guide. Nothing a beginner publisher may read or hear, however, will prove as enlightening as the day-to-day experience of producing the first issue—and for that matter, issues much further down the road. Experience is the best teacher for those who are ready and willing to learn.

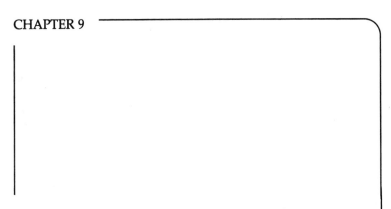

CHAPTER 9

Careers in Business Journalism

There is no prescribed course of study for the business journalist, such as those required in medicine, law, engineering, or public accounting. Successful editors and publishers have come from a variety of backgrounds, some without a college degree. However, with the growth of the business journalism field and with improved standards of excellence and heightened competition, specialized education and training have become increasingly valuable.

A suggested minimal educational program for a business journalist might include a four-year college education with a major in English and a program of study that includes courses in writing and reporting, economics, psychology, and business.

It is also recommended, though, again, not essential, that the student pursue a graduate degree in journalism, usually of one-year's duration, such as those offered by Columbia, Northwestern, Missouri, Syracuse, or New York universities. These institutions and many others also offer four-year degree courses for journalism majors. (See the appendixes for a listing of colleges and universities offering business journalism courses.) Students who pursue journalism as an undergraduate course of study and who plan to make business journalism their career would do well to take a number of business courses, including economics. Still better, a four-year journalism major can benefit considerably from graduate studies in business, such as the master of business administration (MBA) programs offered by Harvard, Stanford, Columbia, or New York universities.

149

If there is an ideal education for a business journalist, it could well be an undergraduate degree in journalism (including courses in the humanities, literature, and pyschology), with a graduate degree in business. As this book is being prepared for printing, the Gallatin Division of New York University is completing plans for the development of a special program on business magazine publishing. It will include courses in various schools and departments of NYU, including journalism, business, psychology, and the humanities. It will be an undergraduate course leading to a B.A. degree, and will include internships with various companies.

Electives in the sciences, particularly chemistry, physics, and mathematics, can also prove worthwhile, especially if the would-be journalist plans to cover scientific and engineering fields, including "high technology."

Regardless of the field of study, the business journalist will find that his or her education really begins the first day of employment. There is no substitute for education on the job.

Internship Programs

An increasing number of schools and departments of journalism are offering internship programs with various business media, and especially with the specialized business press. As an example, Magazines For Industry, Inc., participated in such a program for a number of years with the Department of Journalism of New York University (NYU), as well as NYU's Gallatin Division. The program proved valuable—not only for the interns, but for NYU and MFI.

In one case, a position was available for an associate editor of one of MFI's larger periodicals. One of the interns on the job at that time was doing so well and expressed such interest in making business journalism his career that he was hired for the job. Two years later he was considered the "back-up" to the editor in chief of that publication. This unusual "jump" on the career ladder might not have been offered him had the editors not been confident of his abilities as a result of the internship.

Rewards of Business Press Careers

More often than not, the student preparing for a career in journalism does not consider the business press, both because of lack of publicity about this special area of journalism and because of misconceptions about the field. However, the business press today offers great opportunities for creativity, job fulfillment, and personal growth, and encompasses many more fields and activities than it did not many years ago. The field is endlessly varied and sophisticated, and offers exposure to activities that relate not only to new consumer products and services, but to the interrelationship among many types of people, the arts, government, medicine, and more. To a great extent, the world of business affects just about every phase of human endeavor. It may also not be generally known that business publications represent the single largest segment of special-interest publishing, much larger than the consumer group of special-interest magazines that deal, for example, with photography, music, art, sports, and home furnishing.

The business press also offers many career opportunities that do not directly relate to the editorial function—for example, in circulation, advertising space-selling, art, production, promotion, accounting, and management. Each of these areas can provide significant opportunity for fulfillment and growth.

In addition, with the advent of computerized typesetting, more business magazine companies are purchasing in-house phototypesetting and related equipment, offering new job opportunities for operators and managers of such equipment.

MONETARY REWARDS

Salaries in business magazine publishing now compare favorably with those of many other professions. While a business journalism trainee may start with a salary as low as $10,000 a year, editors in chief, executive editors, and managing editors (for example, of medical journals) now earn annual salaries as high as $75,000. The salaries of editors and advertising personnel in industrial publications range from $35,000 to $50,000 annually.

Advertising sales persons do equally as well, and the salaries of departmental heads compare favorably with departmental and line managers in almost any type of business operation. Those who reach the position of group publishers often earn in excess of $100,000 per year, while heads of major business magazine publishing companies can earn as much as $200,000 a year, and in some instances much more.

Promotions in business periodical publishing occur at a faster rate than in other areas of publishing. This is largely because of the specialized nature of the business press, which encourages promotions from within, and also because most specialized periodical staffs are small enough to allow the able and creative person to grow and advance more swiftly in the staff hierarchy than would be possible in other operations where competition is much more intense.

PART IV

Supplementary Functions of the Business Press

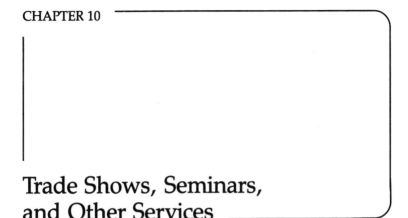

CHAPTER 10

Trade Shows, Seminars, and Other Services

Except for very small companies that have neither adequate staffing nor adequate financing, the business periodical press in the 1970s and 1980s has moved smartly into a number of functions and services that extend considerably beyond publishing. Specialized periodical publishers have entered peripheral fields such as seminars and trade shows; marketing and merchandising services; and, since the early 1980s, the data-base publishing field. As a result, today's business press is providing a growing list of new types of informational services and, at the same time, adding profitable sales volume.

This chapter is devoted to trade shows and seminars, using several publishers as examples. Chapter 11 takes up marketing and merchandising services, and Chapter 12, the newest informational medium, data-base publishing.

Trade Shows and Seminars

So important have seminars and trade shows operated by the business press become that some companies are identified as much by their trade shows and seminars as by the periodicals they publish.

In addition to their image-enhancing capabilities, trade shows and seminars have added considerable revenue to the operations of publishing companies. The receipt of specialized information as a result of questionnaires distributed to registrants is yet another benefit: Trade shows operated by business magazine publishers draw from 8,000 to 50,000 members of an industry served by one or more magazines, providing large-scale possibilities for information gathering.

Operating a trade show clearly complements the work of a business magazine; attendees may subscribe to a magazine published by the sponsoring company; new products and equipment are displayed, often by a magazine's advertisers; and the latest information in the field is shared in seminars. But operating a trade show is highly specialized. Described simplistically, it entails selecting a market to be covered, renting a suitable exposition area, creating a floor plan, producing promotional material, obtaining lists of potential attendees, and offering and selling exposition booths or floor space through direct marketing, telephone, and personal solicitations. Combining all of these, and many other, facets into a smoothly run exposition is a job for experts. No one should attempt a trade show unless he or she either engages a company that specializes in running such shows or retains the services of one or more professional managers.

CAHNERS PUBLISHING COMPANY

Cahners Publishing Company, Boston, one of the largest business magazine publishing operations in the United States, has been extensively involved in creating and managing trade shows. (Southam Communications Limited, a Canadian business publisher headquartered in Toronto, is a second large North American company involved in trade show management.) Cahners, a subsidiary of International Publishing Corporation, Ltd., London, which is in turn a division of the Reed Group of Great Britain, operates 44 domestic shows and 23 international shows, with a combined annual attendance of over three million. The Cahners trade show business continues to grow, generating a substantial part of the company's revenue.

The Cahners Exposition Group includes five other companies around the world which specialize in trade shows; some also publish specialized business magazines. While Cahners owns most of the trade shows it operates, some are managed on a contract basis, usually in conjunction with trade associations which are not only experienced in trade show management, but which cater to the field covered by the show. The Cahners trade shows are highly diversified, covering such fields as hardware, woodworking, computerized office equipment, pharmaceuticals and cosmetics, electronic packaging, printed circuits and micro-electronics, electro-optics/lasers, international telecommunications, naval technology, data communications, and fancy food and confections.

Not unlike other publishers involved in trade shows, Cahners often runs concurrent seminars. A good example is the International Security Conferences and Expositions. Since 1967, in cooperation with Cahners' two magazines in this field, *Security World* and *Security Distributing & Marketing*, the company has been running annual combined conferences and expositions in major cities across the United States. While Cahners directs the exposition program, the two magazines' editors and publishers help in developing the seminar and conference programs.

Often the profits from seminars are greater than those of the concurrent shows, with the earnings of the two averaging, respectively, approximately 60 percent to 40 percent. However, seminars held without a trade show have not proved as successful. It is the combination that makes for a profitable event.

Another lucrative adjunct to running trade shows is the publication of "show dailies." Often business periodicals that do not run a particular trade show will publish a show daily as the official daily of the trade show sponsor. For example, *Food & Drug Packaging* has published a show daily for a number of years during the Packaging Machinery Manufacturers Institute biannual trade show in Chicago. The show is one of the biggest of its kind, drawing an attendance in excess of 40,000. The *Food & Drug Packaging* staff, together with members of other MFI periodicals, produce the show daily like a newspaper. Staffers cover daily activities, writing during the day and delivering manuscript to a Chicago printer before midnight, so that copies can be distributed to the trade show in the morning. The daily carries advertising in each issue.

INDUSTRY MEDIA, INC.

Industry Media, Inc., a U.S. company that publishes, among others, *Plastics Design Forum, Plastics Compounding*, and *Plastics Machinery and Equipment*, decided to enter the trade show field following an intensive study of the demographics of the existing plastics trade show, the National Plastics Exposition, held in Chicago every third year. Industry Media discovered that many potential attendees did not go to the National Plastics Exposition because it was not of particular value to them. Thus, Industry Media decided to launch its own regional Plastics Fair program, but not before surveying its advertisers to determine the desirability of regional shows, as well as to obtain recommendations for suggested locations.

The first Plastics Fair regional trade show was held in January 1980, with several additional shows held since in major cities across the country. The Plastics Fairs, which also feature a seminar program, have proved extremely successful, providing both product exposure and information exchange to complement the work of Industry Media's plastics magazines. To promote the fairs, the magazines publish special show issues, with additional advertising pages. A tabloid periodical, *Plastics Fair News*, which does not carry trade advertising, is also published.

Prior to entering the trade show business, Industry Media had a fully functioning seminar service, which it expanded considerably to incorporate into the Plastics Fair programs. In addition to the fairs, Industry Media now also schedules four seminars in major cities in the United States.

David Cheifetz, president of Conference Management Corporation (hired by Industry Media to assist in planning and managing the Plastics Fair program), believes, and rightly so, that the business magazine publisher has an entrepreneurial tendency to expand beyond print media, and that trade shows, as a natural complement to the "written word," provide magazines with an additional profit center, normally with low up-front risk and fairly high long-term potential.

FOLIO: THE MAGAZINE FOR MAGAZINE MANAGEMENT

One of the most successful trade show/seminar programs to be created in recent years is that sponsored and operated by *Folio: The Magazine for Magazine Management*, owned by Joseph Hanson. (For a description of its Face to Face, Annual Publishing Conference & Exposition, see Chapter 2.) Along with the over 50-year-old *Advertising Age* and the equally long-established *Media and Marketing Decisions*, *Folio* now ranks as one of the top three most successful ventures directed to the media field.

PENTON/IPC, INC.

Penton/IPC, Cleveland, one of the country's largest business magazine companies and a division of the Pittway Corporation, is also in the trade show business. It sponsors a major engineering show through several of its magazines, *Power Transmission Design, Hydraulics & Pneumatics, Precision Metal,* and *Materials Engineering.* This trade show has a gross revenue of over $50,000. A feature of the show is a special "show issue" of each of the sponsoring magazines. Promotion for the show is handled by the combined staffs of the sponsoring magazines.

How far will the specialized business press go in areas beyond publishing periodicals? The horizon seems unlimited. For example, Penton/IPC is now in the fields of real estate and of television programming and production. For example, it owns a resort complex in Florida, which it plans to use as a location for special seminars offered by its periodicals. Businesses also can rent the resort facilities for training, sales meetings, and business conventions. Today, Penton/IPC has an annual business volume in excess of $100 million, and it expects to double this within "a reasonable period." Ancillary activities such as those mentioned above will make this kind of growth possible.

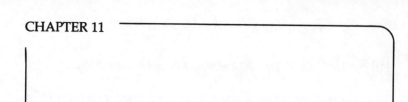

CHAPTER 11

Marketing and Merchandising Services

Most specialized business magazines provide a range of marketing and merchandising services for their advertisers and members of the industries with which they are involved. A small but growing number of companies offer such services through a special marketing and merchandising department.

The basic purpose of such services is to improve the continually growing information flow between the suppliers of an industry and the manufacturers, distributors, and dealers of the industry, beyond that provided by a magazine

Direct mail represents the single largest type of marketing program traditionally made available by the specialized business press, but the list of services has expanded so that it now also includes research projects to determine, for example, market and growth potential for new products, and changes in demographics and taste.

The preparation of advertising is another merchandising service offered by some specialized business magazines. Typically, the magazine works with the advertising agency of a client company, helping the agency to determine the direction its advertising program should take and to ascertain the specialized needs of particular industries.

Other merchandising services include convention and exposition group trips, especially when such gatherings are held in foreign countries; plant visits, usually directed by the technical editor of the magazine involved; and the publication of contract books on subjects of interest to industry suppliers.

160

Direct Mail

Of all the services provided by the specialized press, direct mail is the most widely promoted and used. The basic purpose of direct mail is to help a supplier place its sales message in the hands of sales prospects or of those in a position to influence such sales. Though specific strategies differ according to the industries, markets, and the publications providing the service, the basic methodologies are the same.

Publications offering direct-mail services take great care in building and maintaining their specialized mailing lists. A customer purchasing the right to use such lists can thus specify whether he or she desires the total list of the publication (such as a list of producers of steel, plastics, or computer hardware) or a smaller, more select list of executives designated by function. Most specialized publications have complete computerized breakdowns of their subscription lists, which are updated periodically to provide "freshness" for "renters" of their direct mail services. Selectivity in such lists is usually based on SIC (Standard Industrial Classification) classification, job function, plant (or other business) size, product category, geographic breakdown and zip codes, and/or any combination desired.

As explained earlier, publications never sell their lists as such. What they "sell" is the right to *use* them. Rental is a better word. Lists are the "life blood" of a publication, and thus publishers take no chance that their lists will fall into the hands of competitors. Of course, suppliers can buy lists from professional list firms, but the quality and specificity of these do not compare with updated lists from publications.

Rental rates can be as low as $20 per 1,000 names or as high as $100 per 1,000 names, depending on how specialized the lists are and the costs involved in developing and maintaining them. As a rule, magazine advertisers receive a discount. Most publications have a minimum charge for each mailing or program of mailing.

Normally, the supplier renting a list arranges to deliver the material to be mailed to the publication's mailing house, which then does the actual mailing to the list specified. Most publications require that a sample of the mailing piece (or pieces) be submitted to assure that the mailing meets certain standards.

The publication ordinarily guarantees its lists, and refunds the postage cost of mail that is returned from the post office (usually not more than 3 to 5 percent of the total mailed). Advertising agencies ordering lists for their clients are normally qualified to receive the standard 15 percent agency commission of the cost of the list rental.

Southam Communications Limited provides an example of a company that has developed a substantial and sophisticated marketing program, of which direct marketing is a major component:

- Direct Mail—This service is provided by Southam Direct Marketing services through plants in Toronto, Montreal, and Ottawa. In addition to renting all company publications' lists, Southam offers others that the company develops. It also provides complete in-plant mail handling services other than graphic production and printing. It provides, as well, a fulfillment service for external clients who require coupon redemption and premium and sampling fulfillment.
- Direct Response Marketing—This department offers for sale, usually on a mail-order basis, a wide variety of technical and general books for people in business and the professions. In addition, a number of adult learning programs are sold. Plans are underway to broaden the scope of this department.
- Building Reports—This is an information service for suppliers in the construction business, offering information and progress reports on, for example, contemplated building projects, as well as other services, including lists of engineers and contractors, and copies of contractors' bid specifications. This information is provided by the Southam Building Reports' Construction News Service.
- Telephone Marketing—This service consists of telephone activities, which are combined with the company's direct mail promotion and advertising to produce inquiries and orders.

Publishing Technical and Other Specialized Books

The publishing of specialized books is a valuable service offered industry by the specialized business press. Obviously not all such publishers issue books, but the number that do is increasing, and many are expanding their list of titles. Some of the larger business magazine publishers have separate book departments with their own staffs; most medium-size companies use existing staff from other departments, however. Following is a description, first, of how a medium-size magazine publishing company handles its book operation, followed by a description of one large company's book department.

Magazines For Industry, Inc., has published books almost since its inception in 1944. The books have been published by its various magazine groups (i.e., profit centers); for example, there are publications on candy production, glass manufacture, packaging, dairy production, and beverage marketing. Each profit center is under the direction of the division publisher and utilizes the company's service departments, such as production, art, circulation, direct mail, and accounting.

When a book is published, promotional material is usually mailed to potential buyers prior to publication. Normally, enough orders are received before publication to cover the cost of printing and binding of the initial run, usually no more than 3,000 copies, only half of which are bound at publication.

Magazines For Industry is one of a growing number of specialized business publishers which publish books for supply firms under contract. A good example is *Packaging in Today's Society*, a paperback published for the St. Regis Paper Co., New York. MFI produced the book for St. Regis on a cost-plus basis, which afforded MFI a fair profit.

Southam Communications' book publishing department includes numerous medical books, including *The Canadian Medical Directory*, a compilation of some 45,000 physicians in Canada, along with listings of health care institutions. Also part of Southam's book department is its Sales Management Systems service, which provides computerized territory management and call-reporting systems to the pharmaceutical industry. A spin-off service, called Adrep, provides a detailed monthly summary of advertising, by categories of pharmaceutical products, in Canada's national medical journals.

HBJ Publications has a separate book division which publishes and markets books created by the staffs of its various publications. Thus, this phase of the business is centralized.

CHAPTER 12

Data-Base and Electronic Publishing: The New Challenge

At the 1980 annual meeting of the American Business Press in Chicago, Robert M. O'Hara, senior vice president of the Mead Corporation, Dayton, Ohio, one of the country's major producers of paper products, including publication print paper, devoted the majority of his speech to data-base publishing and how this new electronic form of information storage and retrieval can be used to advantage by the business press. O'Hara is also president of Mead's Advanced Systems Group, which includes the corporation's substantial and profitable data-base project, launched in 1972.

O'Hara explained that Mead's entry into high-technology information marketing was precipitated by the realization that the growth of the print paper business is expected to level off in the eighties and nineties and may well decline in the years beyond, while the future of data-base marketing seems unlimited. Thus, Mead hopes to assure a place for itself in a new medium of communication that offers tremendous growth potential.

The first project of Mead Data Central, as its data-base program is called, was the development of a data base for the legal profession that has now become the leading legal-information retrieval service in the country.

O'Hara urged the assembled business magazine publishers to enter the data-base publishing field. Increasingly, he stated, companies are moving beyond the traditional world of publishing, investing rather in the broader "information marketing business," with trade shows, seminars, marketing and technical services—and services based on a computerized data base.

Definition of Data Base

What is a data base? Simply stated, it represents a fund of specialized information that, once fed into a computer, may be retrieved in a variety of ways. Every publisher has on hand a base of valuable information. To develop an electronic data base for such printed information, including specialized circulation lists, all that is needed is for publishers to develop a data-base program, acquire the needed software; and lease, share, or work out a joint venture to acquire necessary computer hardware.

It should be pointed out that data-base publishing (though not by that name) is not new. For years, publishers of business magazines and other periodicals have successfully marketed different types of information or media developed from a single pool of information. However, electronic data processing makes this information quickly storable, retrievable, and marketable. Moreover—and this is key— technology makes it possible to connect the data base directly to production machinery, whether this is another computer, typesetting equipment, typewriters, teletype networks, television screens, or even electronically produced voices. Even invoicing and bill paying can be done electronically.

An increasing number of specialized business periodical publishers are entering or moving toward electronic data-base publishing. McGraw-Hill, Inc., the largest of these, has entered the market through the acquisition of Data Resources, Inc. (for $100 million) and has thus begun to build a substantial data-base business. Before the end of the eighties, it is anticipated that most of the established business magazine publishing firms will be involved in electronic data-base publishing.

Examples of Data-Base Services

Electronic data-base business publishing has almost unlimited potential. Here are just a few examples of the types of information a publishing company can make available to its data-base subscribers, advertisers, or other buyers.

- By the time an article is published in a periodical, much research has gone into its development; the background material may contain many more words than the article itself. The data base of the article will include not only the article itself but most, if not all, of the research material. A data-base buyer can request any part of such material for his or her own research.
- Many business magazines regularly publish interviews with executives. Such interviews may have a common denominator, such as marketing trends in a particular industry. The data base could include the questions asked and answers given in all such interviews, offering a quick marketing overview to interested buyers.
- Publishers of specialized business magazines often issue annual directories of manufacturers and products, as well as a "who's who" of sales and marketing executives, plus demographics of all kinds. Updated material of this kind can be included in a publisher's electronic data base.
- Business magazine publishers make periodic studies of market trends. With such material in the data base, a buyer or subscriber can compare market trends of specific types of products and brands with the sales trends of his or her own products.
- Almost all business periodicals publish news of executive appointments and personnel movements in an industry. With such material in a data base, a buyer or subscriber can rapidly obtain information about a particular executive or about trends in personnel changes and movements.
- A magazine about developments in food products (or other fast evolving products) can develop a highly specialized data bank on product research, product development trends, the introduction of new products, those that succeeded and to what extent, and those that failed and for what reasons.

No matter what data-base services are eventually offered, the key to success will be found in the software. A data-base program must allow information to be updated and expanded, in order to assure its continued accuracy and relevance.

So important has the data-base field become that publishers who fail to develop a data base exploiting their own informational capabilities run the risk of being pre-empted by computer-oriented entrepreneurs.

What the Mead Corporation did with its Lexis data-base program for the legal profession, the initial business of its Mead Data Central (MDC), for example, could and should have been done by a law journal or other legally oriented magazine. In fact, Mead made a serious effort to engage the services of a law journal in a joint venture but failed: The publishers of the legal periodicals maintained that there was no market for the service. They were wrong. In 1979, Mead earned $4.2 million (of about $50 million in revenue of MDC) and reported that this was merely a beginning.

In an interview in the March 1981 issue of *Media Management Monographs*, Paul F. McPherson, then president, now executive vice president of McGraw-Hill Publications Company, a division of McGraw-Hill, Inc., was interviewed by Jim Mann, publisher of *Media Management Monographs*. Data-base information marketing, according to Mann, who uses the term very broadly, comprises three media categories: print (books, magazines, etc.), "face to face" (through conferences and seminars), and electronic (information retrieved and transmitted via a computer). McPherson ultimately envisions multimedia information enterprises—a mass of data organized and made available by a publisher, with the choice of the medium dependent on the market. As an example of the exploitation of electronic media, McGraw-Hill has developed a teletype message service for subscribers in the petrochemical market. In addition, McGraw-Hill, through its Data Resources Inc., provides (among other things) electronic economic models on the macroeconomy, which subscribers can use to develop individual business scenarios on their own terminal.

As Mann points out in a later analysis of the interview, there is a distinction between the theory and practice of data-base publishing. While it makes enormous sense in theory to build a multimedia enterprise, in practice, he says, "we know of no company where the mass of data, or data base, came first. Data bases are always organized by publishers initially to develop a single medium, e.g., a specific magazine. The idea of using the data base to develop other media is almost always an afterthought."

Will Data-Base Publishing Replace Magazines?

Will data-base publishing eventually replace magazines? The answer, according to McPherson, is a definite *no*. Magazines and other forms of print media will survive because their function and appeal (presenting information in a manner that allows for leisurely reading and in a format that is pleasing both to the eye and to the touch) cannot be duplicated by electronics. On the other hand, a periodical cannot duplicate the computer's ability to manipulate large amounts of data, retrieve information for a specific purpose, or combine information on hand with information in the data base. Far from competing with magazines, data-base publishing complements them—each "feeding" information to the other.

Pointers for Setting Up a Data-Base Program

Finally, Mann, as part of his analysis of the interview, offered the following five pointers for publishers who plan to set up a data-base program:

1. *Don't invest in tools simply because they intrigue you.* For the publishers, both a data base and a computer are tools. Both are expensive to obtain and maintain. Successful publishers invest in them only if probability of returns justifies cost.

2. *Evaluate the data base you now have.* Every publisher already has—and is using—some sort of data base, even if it is only the back issues of the magazine. What is that material worth and to whom? How can it be reused?

Data already collected may be useful in a data-base program if it is supplemented by and combined with other information. Ask the questions: How feasible is it to add such material? And, will the product that can be generated from the altered data base justify the cost of the alterations?

It is important also to look beyond the editorial data base. For example, the subscriber-information data base developed by the circulation department, or the market-research data base created for the advertising sales force, may be as or more valuable than the editorial data base—and more easily computerized.

3. *Be very specific in each new use for a data base.* When you market information, the medium is the message. From a marketing viewpoint, information is much like food: customers want it processed. Thus, information marketers do not sell information; they sell books, magazines, cassettes, records, wire services, electronic access, etc.

The data base will have to be adjusted and manipulated for each new medium. Hence, it is essential that publishers envision a new medium with precision, not only in physical terms (books, magazines, cassettes, etc.), but in terms of the way it will be marketed and used. In most cases, publishers will find, other factors being equal, that it is advisable to adopt a medium that requires the least changes in the data base.

4. *Let present customers lead you to future products.* Marketers of information have a tremendous advantage. The communications business, by its very nature, generates feedback full of new product ideas. Listen to your readers. Watch them.

What happens after the readers receive your magazine? Are the issues stored for reference, torn up, passed on, reproduced? How frequent are requests for additional information? In what areas? Are readers meshing your material with other information and restructuring it for special uses? Can you publish information in a form that would make such uses easier for them?

Does your publication have a secondary market other than your primary readers? Would tailoring the same information to produce a medium primarily for them make sense?

Are there aspects of your publication that inadequately meet the needs of your readers, e.g., news you provide weekly that they could use daily, leads that would be more useful if qualified, print that needs illustrations, illustrations that need to be more compelling? Every well-run publication engages in this constant analysis of how well it fulfills readers' needs. It takes a farsighted publisher, however, to envision answers beyond the potential of the magazine itself. This requires the ability to think entirely in terms of market needs, free of preconceptions about specific media forms.

5. *Learn as much about computers as you can.* Computers and computer technology have become as important to publishing as printing processes, distribution methods, and promotion techniques. In some instances, though, publishers would be well advised, at least for the present, to let someone else put all or part of the data base on the computer. In other instances, computerizing a data base may be worthwhile purely for internal purposes, e.g., to produce more accurate or thorough editorial data or to organize data more effectively for readers.

It is crucial to point out that while any number of firms, such as Mead Corporation, can move to develop a specialized data base, few organizations can do so with as much potential for success as publishers of specialized periodicals. This is so not only because publishers have a built-in data base in the form of their magazines, but also because publishers may rely on the expertise of their editorial staffs, without whom it is extremely difficult to develop a meaningful and useful data base. The specialized business periodical has the information *and* the editorial talent to develop, interpret, and format a data base quickly and effectively.

Electronic Publishing

One of the newest forms of activity for the specialized press, and one that could be operated in conjunction with data-base publishing, is electronic publishing. This is the delivery of business news of a specialized nature through the electronic media instead of or supplementary to print media. *The Wall Street Journal* has been the forerunner in this area; some of the larger business publishers such as McGraw-Hill are also moving in this direction.

Both data-base and electronic publishing were the subjects of a two-day seminar held in 1980, and sponsored by the Knowledge Industry Publications, Inc., of White Plains, N.Y. (This com-

pany started in 1977 and publishes specialized business magazines and newsletters such as *Video User* and *Sporting Commercials*.)
The seminar was titled "The Print Publisher in an Electronic
World." One of the most insightful presentations, included in a
subsequent seminar report, was made by Joseph I. Dionne, executive vice president, operations, at McGraw-Hill, Inc. His topic
was "How a Diversified Publisher Looks at Electronics."

For McGraw-Hill, developing and marketing a data-base
program was comparatively easy, since McGraw-Hill already had
several information "bases," with the accompanying expertise.
These were represented by the company's four specialized information divisions: Standard & Poor; McGraw-Hill Publications,
Inc.; McGraw-Hill Book Company; and the Information Systems
Company. The move to data-base publishing was not without its
share of problems, however, largely because at that time (1975)
it was difficult to locate individuals with direct experience in the
area. Nevertheless, four executives, each from within the afore-
mentioned divisions, were eventually located and placed under
the direction of a senior management executive of the corporation.

Here is a summary of Dionne's prescription for the successful launching of an electronic publishing venture:

- Senior management understanding of and commitment to
  the precepts of data-base publishing
- The creation of the infrastructure of market research and
  product development capability, as well as efficient data-base
  management and special knowledge of and facility with the
  technology involved
- The need for product champions
- Open and frequent discussions to penetrate an environment
  that has rigid routines
- The need to be comfortable with multiple-discipline input
  as a result of the new technologies involved
- The capacity to resolve problematic issues and the need for
  a flexible environment that will permit such issues to surface
- The need for an entirely new look at the complete marketing
  and sales support systems area

And, finally, a great deal of patience.

Data-base publishing is just one example of the kind of exciting information-marketing projects that the specialized business press will increasingly be involved in. Business journalism offers unlimited potential for exploiting new approaches to disseminating information.

PART V

Public Relations and Advertising in Business Communications

CHAPTER 13

Corporate Communicators and the Role of Professional Societies

In a July 1980 article in *Industrial Marketing*, Editor Bob Donath said: "Corporate communications, at times a poorly defined step-child of corporate top management, is due for a change in the 1980s." Change is indeed called for. But it will be more evolutionary than drastic, accompanying the changing needs of the corporate structure.

A corporate communicator's job has traditionally involved and will continue to involve at least three major functions: 1) regular communications with the corporations's stockholders, 2) communications with the general public through consumer media (both public relations and advertising), and 3) communications with the business community (again, through public relations and advertising) in both the general and specialized business press.

Training of the Corporate Communicator

Who is the corporate communicator? More often than not, he or she is not a single person but several: a marketing vice president, a financial executive, the advertising manager, and the public relations director. Increasingly in recent years, the communications expertise of the latter three individuals has been combined into one position, that of the director of communications, with a staff of specialists who can deal effectively with shareholders, the financial community (including security analysts), the consumer, and the overall business community. Typically, the director of communications for a large public corporation is a trained journalist with experience and ability in the world of business. As is the case for the specialized business editor, an undergraduate journalism major with a master of business administration (MBA) degree from a top university appears to create the "ideal" candidate for a corporate director of communications, although there are exceptions.

Goals of Corporate Communications

The communication goals of most big corporations are similar. In the case of stockholder relations, the basic purpose is to inform them about what special activities the corporation is involved in, how the company is faring in the marketplace, current sales and profits, and what may be expected in the future. Some of this information is contained in the corporation's annual report as well as in quarterly reports.

Communications with the general public are usually directed through the public relations department or a professional public relations company employed by the corporation (and working in conjunction with its own public relations department). The major goal here is to shed favorable light on the work of the corporation. If the corporation's products are consumer-oriented, this function becomes particularly critical. The corporation also wants the public to buy its stock and/or bonds. The work of communicating with the general public is accomplished primarily through press releases, through the placement of feature stories and interviews in both the consumer and business press, and through a program of corporate advertising (distinct from product advertising).

Sometimes corporate communication with the public takes on urgent importance—for example, when petroleum corporations tried to explain excessively high oil prices and shortages following actions by the Organization of Petroleum Exporting Countries (OPEC) in 1973, or when those industries involved in nuclear-power technology tried to combat antinuclear sentiments following the Three Mile Island incident. Actions taken to try to overcome negative public attitudes included press releases, article placement, and advertising—and corporations found that the task had to be ongoing.

Communicating with the business community, the third aspect of a communications director's job, involves developing a continuing series of public relations "tools" to tell the story of the corporation's programs, goals, and growth formula. These "tools" normally include press releases, feature articles, interviews, and corporate advertising in the business press, both specialized and general, with emphasis on the former.

Specialized business periodicals continue to be the major medium used for communicating with the business community. This is because they provide high-quality coverage, which in turn has produced increased readership among the executives. However, the general business press, which continues to improve its business news coverage and has increased its contact with the leading corporations, is also getting a good share of the corporate advertising budget.

As has been discussed, the daily press is also becoming increasingly aggressive in its business coverage, although in a selective and consumer-oriented manner. While the daily press cannot yet compete with the expertise and detailed coverage of the business press, its aim is to obtain a portion of the corporate advertising budget.

The electronic media, especially television, are also making an attempt to improve business coverage. It is doubtful that they will catch up with print media in the foreseeable future—unless major changes occur in their perceptions of what prime time audiences are interested in.

In addition to working directly with the print media, corporate communicators cooperate with associations (largely located in Washington, D.C.), helping them to present a positive image of industry. Most industry-related associations, such as those involved with steel, glass manufacturing, aluminum, petroleum, packaging and packaging machinery, food manufacturing, dairy, sugar, and peanuts, employ business-trained journalists and do a creditable job of performing their basic function—acquainting the public, industry, and legislators with the products made and services offered by the industries they represent.

Without the help of corporate communicators, however, they could not function as well as they do. Like the industries they represent, such associations also face public relations problems, such as those that have developed in oil, nuclear energy, sugar, and steel. Associations must be constantly alert and prepared to deal with changing public perceptions, and corporate communicators often provide vital knowledge and know-how.

Business/Professional Advertising Association

Among the association and professional societies that play a major role in business communications is the Business/Professional Advertising Associations (B/PAA). The B/PAA is a 60-year-old group with over 3,200 members in advertising, marketing communications, and other marketing professions, working in companies engaged in business-to-business selling, in advertising agencies serving such companies, on business magazines, and with firms that provide consulting and/or supporting services.

Most members of the B/PAA belong to one or more of the group's 32 local chapters in the United States and Canada. Membership is on an individual rather than a company basis. The basic purpose of the B/PAA is to improve professionalism at all levels for all business communicators.

Although an important function of members of the B/PAA is to create and help place industrial advertising for their companies, their larger goal is to function optimally as business communicators. In a 1980 report to the B/PAA membership, Fred C. Poppe, then B/PAA president, stated:

> "In my travels I have found that the B/PAA'ers are getting more and more involved in not just creating better advertising but in coordinating all their communication efforts more professionally. And this is really what the bottom line is in our business. Our management insists on having us produce better forms of communications with better copy, better design, better graphics and,

where appropriate, for use in better media. Therefore, what we produce for our clients and our companies will gain more potential buyers per dollar than our competitors."

To enhance the professionalism of its membership, B/PAA offers a program of certification called the Certified Business Communicator, which provides an incentive for business/professional marketing communications people to continue their professional development and to demonstrate their professional competence.

Public Relations Society of America, Inc.

Another organization that has exerted a major influence on business communications is the Public Relations Society of America, Inc. Public relations, both as a business and a profession, has continued to gain status over the years, so that today staffs, salaries, and budgets are bigger than ever, particularly in the major public corporations. Here one finds public relations executives with a variety of titles: corporate communicator; vice president of corporate affairs or of public affairs; director of communications; and in some cases, director of marketing, with a special office of public relations and communications.

The Public Relations Society of America, Inc., was organized in 1947 to assist public relations professionals in improving their skills and to set standards for professional practice. Today, with a membership of approximately 10,000, it is the largest PR organization in the world. Society members come from advertising agencies, business and industry, public relations counseling firms, government agencies, educational institutions, trade and professional groups, hospitals, and other nonprofit organizations. The Society has a Code of Professional Standards for the Practice of Public Relations, backed by enforcement procedures, to which all members are required to adhere.

While no special educational requirements are prescribed for membership in the Society, most members are college graduates, a large number being graduates of schools or departments of journalism; some have completed additional courses in public relations, and a smaller number have earned MBAs.

The Society has a program of continuing education (through its various chapters) by which it encourages and assists local colleges and universities in providing adult education courses in public relations techniques and management. Through affiliate membership in the American Council on Education for Journalism and other similar alliances, the Society also increases the scope of its educational activities and participates in the accreditation of college public relations courses.

In addition, the Society helps prepare young people for careers in public relations by its sponsorship of the Public Relations Student Society, which has a membership of about 3,000 students on about 80 college campuses and universities.

In 1964, the Society established a voluntary Accreditation Program, which offers members an opportunity to take written and oral examinations to demonstrate their knowledge of and competence in the practice of public relations.

With headquarters in New York, the Society's various services include a research information center, its *Public Relations Journal*, the *PRSA National Newsletter*, and the annual *Public Relations Register*. The Society works with the media and various organizations to gain understanding of public relations, and also maintains liaisons with public information officers in a variety of federal, state, and local government departments and agencies to provide governmental and legislative information for Society members.

Status of Public Relations in the Corporate World

Beginning salaries in public relations differ little from those in other branches of journalism. As of 1982, entry salaries were approximately $10,000 to $12,000 per year. However, advancement is often swift, and for those hired at a management level, the remuneration may be $50,000 or more per year.

Often, the public relations field draws applicants from the media, particularly the specialized business press and consumer magazines. However, because of the special pressures found in public relations, such personnel often return to their original medium, but generally to more important positions as a result of their public relations experience.

What is the future of the editorial employee in public relations? He or she could join a large advertising agency or public corporation, eventually moving up to the directorship. The employee could also eventually start a public relations company, or become a magazine publisher. All of these routes have been followed. The public relations field offers exciting, if sometimes hectic, experience, which can prove valuable for writers, editors, and other communicators who eventually make their future in the media field. Generally, the staff turnover in public relations is much heavier than in media.

In early 1981, *Advertising Age* devoted a 12-page section to public relations, including a listing of the fifty largest public relations companies—from Hill & Knowlton, the leader with a 1980 fee income of $34,775,564 and 800 employees, to Bob Thomas & Associates, the smallest of the fifty, with fee income for 1980 of $696,935 and 22 employees. Hill & Knowlton showed a gain of 22 percent while Bob Thomas's increase amounted to just under 5 percent. The largest gains for 1980 were reported by Fleishman-Hillard, eighteenth on the list, with fee income of $2,745,346, and Woody Kepner Associates, fortieth, with fee income of $947,096. Each showed a gain of 47.8 percent.

While public relations has become "big business," only the ten largest firms had annual revenues in excess of $5 million. However, public relations firms do not produce products. It is strictly a people business, with salaries representing the big annual item of cost.

In *Advertising Age*'s lead article, entitled "Skills Needed, Status Growing," B.G. Yovovich calls attention to a number of forces that have increased the importance of public relations. Two of these are the rising cost of advertising and the proliferation of media outlets. The rising cost of advertising, Yovovich explains, has benefited those marketing public relations, as well as those using publicity and nonadvertising communications to achieve marketing goals. And, as mentioned earlier in this chapter and supported in this article, the increase in media outlets (and the greater emphasis on business news in all forms of media) has brought about "a voracious appetite for editorial material" to which public relations professionals are responding widely and effectively.

In the same article, Yovovich quotes Denny Griswold, founder and editor of the *Public Relations Newsletter*, on the growth and accepted values of public relations:

> "If you study the history of American business you will see that the leadership always responds to the needs of the time. There was a time when production was king. When marketing grew in importance, salesmen took over. During the anti-trust era, the financial man and lawyer were on top. Today, public relations skills are what is called for, and public relations is achieving a status in the corporate world comparable to production, marketing, finance, and law."

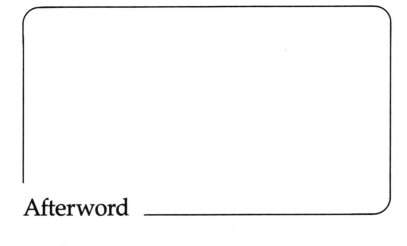

Afterword

What is the future of business journalism? With the information explosion so all-encompassing and unpredictable, it is perhaps more difficult now than at any other time in business press history to make predictions. Nevertheless, if the increasing need for highly specialized information and the burgeoning technology for delivering such information are reliable indicators, the growth potential of the business press, and particularly the specialized business periodical, appears unlimited.

In 1980, the School of Journalism of the University of Missouri issued a report entitled "Communication 1990," which was the work of a special Future Committee consisting of faculty members, a graduate student in journalism, and members of the media. On the subject of the future of magazines, including the specialized business press, the report stated:

> "Projecting the state of the magazine industry as far as 1990 would be a difficult and dangerous mission at any time. In the present state of our economy prediction is even more difficult.
>
> "Nonetheless, no one in any area of the magazine business predicts anything but a continuing boom. The basic reason is simply this: A highly individualized population seeking personal fulfillment will demand a more and more highly specialized form of communication. Magazines and their stepchild, newsletters, fill the bill."

In my opinion, this prediction is particularly telling for the future of specialized business periodicals. While such magazines are currently facing increased competition—from large daily

185

neswpapers, from general business magazines, from news weeklies, and from other consumer magazines directed to specialized
interests—they still respond to the informational needs of industry in a way that no other type of publication can. Specialized
business publications are not only closest to the "action" in business and industry, but their content is much more comprehensive, and their staffs are uniquely qualified to cover business and
industry. No ambitious industry executive can expect to be fully
informed of developments and trends without regularly reading
specialized periodicals.

The specialized business press, for its part, must assure that
it is constantly alert to the changing needs of industry by hiring
and promoting the best available talent, by utilizing the latest
production technology, by superior management practices, and—
as is already being demonstrated in high-technology fields such
as computers and electronics—by introducing new magazines
(or segmenting existing ones) to cover new and emerging industries. Informational needs in many areas of business and industry, but especially in high-technology fields, have proved so vast
and so urgent that only highly specialized business periodicals
have been able to keep pace. (Textbooks, for example, quickly
become dated, and conferences and seminars cannot be organized fast enough.) To deal with the problems and opportunities
posed by such informational needs, specialized business periodicals must continue to institute training programs for editors
and other personnel, as well as to develop new approaches to
capital formation and to the judicious use of existing (and new)
revenue sources.

There is no way to know at this time where the developing
communications technologies will lead. But one thing is certain:
There is no end in sight.

It has been demonstrated again and again that whenever a
great need develops, the concepts and methodology necessary
to fill that need are created and developed. The need for specialized business information will not only continue but increase.

Unquestionably, data-base and electronic publishing will play
an important role in business communications of the future, with
a substantial segment of their source material emanating from
the specialized business press. In no way, however, will they replace

the value and appeal of print media. There is nothing available today or planned in the future that can directly or indirectly replace the printed word, whether it is in the daily newspaper, magazine, newsletter, or the general or specialized business periodical.

The future of business journalism is thus assured. In present as well as in new forms . . . with new approaches and with new excitement . . . with an unlimited growth.

Appendixes

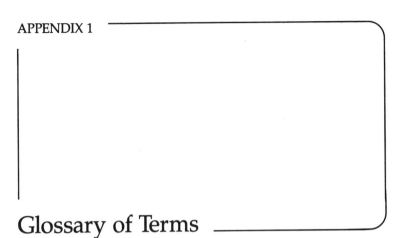

Glossary of Terms

AA   Author's alterations.

Benday   Film or other type of proof with a screen pattern of half-tone dots or lines that provide varied tonal effect.

Bleed   Illustrations both for editorial and advertising that run off one or more of the edges of the page and are partially trimmed off when page is cut for binding.

Blues (Blueline)   A photoprint made from a negative; used as a final proof before a publication goes to press.

Break Up   To separate lengthy material into shorter paragraphs.

Brownprint, Vandyke   Type of print used as a proof for halftones.

Camera-Ready Copy   Final proofs from which negatives generally are made; used in offset printing.

Caption   Heading of a chapter or article, or explanatory material accompanying an illustration.

Character   A numeral or a letter of the alphabet; a symbol used in type.

Character Count   A count of each letter, numeral, symbol, or punctuation mark in the body of copy.

Cold Type Composition   Process of setting type by a direct-impression method or a typewriter composing machine; done without the casting of hot metal. Not to be confused with phototypography.

Collate   To assemble sheets or signatures of printed matter in correct numerical order.

Color Separation   The separation of colors of a transparency into different color filters, each of which will be reproduced by a separate printing plate carrying a color.

Compose   To arrange or set letters or numerals of type or film.

Computer Composition   Tape produced on a word processor and run through a computer, with decisions and selections made on the basis of a programmed input. This is the new and soon to become standard way of composing type for layout and printing.

Condensed Type   Typeface that is narrow in proportion to its height.

Copy   Material given to a compositor to be typeset. Can also refer to pictures, photographs, artwork.

Crop   To eliminate parts of a photograph to obtain a desired size or emphasis.

Dead Matter   Material no longer required for printing.

Delete   To eliminate.

Display Type   Print designed for headings and advertisements that is generally larger than the text and designed to attract attention.

Dummy   A preliminary drawing or layout showing the position of illustrations and text as they are to appear in the final reproduction.

Duotone   A two-color halftone reproduction made from a one-color photograph.

Edition   Copies of a book or magazine that have been printed from the same plates.

Folded and Gathered   Pages folded and collected into the correct numerical order for binding.

Folio(s)   A page number; page numbers. Total pages of magazine prior to printing.

Font   A complete assortment of type of one size and face, including caps, lower case, punctuation marks, etc.

Form   A press sheet that contains pages of a book or magazine in the order they are to be printed, prior to final folding and trimming.

Format   The outward appearance, arrangement, and binding of a periodical. Style established for a magazine.

Four-Color   A printing process that prints four colors (yellow, magenta, cyan, and black) on a sheet of paper.

Galley   In "hot type," a shallow metal tray used to hold type. Also, a proof (made either from type on a galley tray or type produced in photocomposition, for example) before the type is made up in pages.

Halftone   A reproduction of continuous tone artwork, such as a photograph, with the image formed by dots of various sizes.

Heading   Headline or title at the beginning of a chapter or sections of a chapter.

Imposition   The laying out of pages in a press form so that they will be in the correct order after the printed sheet is folded.

Insert   A specially printed piece usually prepared for insertion in a publication.

Justification   To set and space lines of type so that all lines fill a uniform width on the page.

Kill   To permanently delete copy or typeset material. Copy originally set for one issue but held over for another issue is termed "overset" copy.

Layout   A rough outline prepared to scale and showing the general appearance of the job to be printed. A "comprehensive" layout is more fully detailed.

Line Copy   Any copy—for example, a pen and ink drawing— that is suitable for reproduction without using a screen.

Line Cut   Photoengraving without any gradations of tone.

Logo   The trademark of a company to be used for its products or business name.

Makeready   The preparation of plates for printing.

Makeup   The arrangement of lines of composed type and also illustrations into pages of proper length.

Masthead   The statement of a newspaper or magazine that includes its name, terms, ownership, platform, and policies. In newspapers, the masthead generally appears on the editorial page; in magazines it usually accompanies the table of contents. Also refers to a newspaper's name, displayed on the first page.

Measure   The width of a line of type on a page.

Mechanical   A page or layout prepared as an original for photomechanical reproduction. Also called a "pasteup."

Offset   Transferring ink that is still wet to the next sheet laid over it. Also called "set off."

Offset Lithography   Printing process in which an inked impression from a plate is first made on a rubber-blanketed cylinder and then transferred to the paper being printed.

Pasteup   The arrangement of type and art into page layouts that will be reproduced mechanically. Also called a "mechanical."

PE   Printer's error.

Photoengraving   A photomechanical process for making line cuts (see above) and halftone cuts (see above) by photographing an image on a metal plate and then etching.

Phototypesetting   Method of composing type in which text and headlines are keyed directly onto film for photographic reproduction.

Phototypography   Term used to denote the field of composing and processing type by phototypesetting. Synonym for photocomposition.

Pica   Printer's unit of measurement generally used in measuring the length of lines. One pica equals 1/6-inch.

Plate   Any surface carrying a reproduced illustration or type form to be used in printing; also an illustration printed separately and inserted into a periodical.

Progressive Proofs   In color separation, a series of proofs of a color-process reproduction pulled in each color and in combinations of two, three, and four colors. Used to indicate color quality and as a guide for printing.

Proofreaders' Marks   Symbols used to indicate errors or changes in text.

Reproduction Proof   Proof of type, on high-quality paper, suitable for photographic reproduction (by a printer). Also called "repro proof."

Reverse   Process of printing in which the parts that are usually black or shaded are reversed, so as to appear white or gray.

Signature   In web printing and binding, the name given to a printed sheet after it has been folded.

Slugs   In "hot type," small pieces of lead that are used as spacing material. In composition, a one-piece line of type.

Space Out   To increase the spacing between words or lines to make full length, or to cover a specified area.

Stripping   Putting together of positive and negative elements in film reproduction.

Thumbnail   An accurate facsimile of a proposed publication, with all components indicated on each page, i.e., copy, illustrations, advertisements, color, advertisers' key numbers, etc.

Trafficking   Processing of advertisers' contracts and insertion orders, and the transfer of all material from advertising agency to printer.

Typographical Error or Typo   An error made by the typesetter. Also called printer's error (PE).

Widow   A short line appearing at the top of a page, or a single word in a line by itself ending a paragraph.

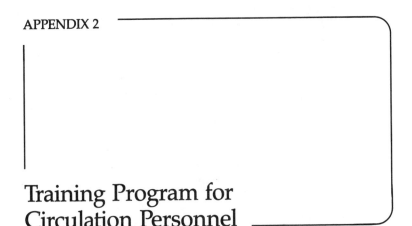

APPENDIX 2

Training Program for Circulation Personnel

CIRCULATION CLASSIFICATIONS

I. CONTROLLED (FREE) CIRCULATION. Primarily for business, professional, and trade (vertical-audience) publications. The editorial content relates to a particular industry.

1. Qualification Requirements. Subscribers receive free copies of each issue if they meet the publication's definitions of recipient qualification and field served. There is as well a required qualification period.

    Maximum qualification period for domestic, Canadian, and European subscriptions is three years; five years for foreign circulation other than Canadian and European.

    Most publications maintain either a one- or two-year qualification period, depending on the cost and competition. Advertisers generally prefer the one-year qualification period, since it provides them with a greater audience for their products or services.

2. Qualification Sources
    a. Personal written request from recipient. Letters from individually qualified recipients requesting the publication.
    b. Written request from recipient's firm. Return of a questionnaire; or a letter on a company letterhead identifying the employee (by name and/or function) and requesting the publication.
    c. Written communication from recipient or recipient's firm (other than request). Same as above, but without the specific request to receive the publication.

        d. Other sources than above. Association rosters and directories; business directories; independent field reports (Dun & Bradstreet, etc.); licensees: federal, state, or local government; manufacturer, distributor, and wholesaler lists; telephone interviews either by publisher's personnel or independent organization.

    3. Preferred Qualified Recipient. The most desirable qualified recipient from an advertiser's point of view is generally source (a) above, and is qualified within a one- year period.

II.   PAID CIRCULATION. Applicable to consumer horizontal-audience publications.

    1. Sources. Subscriptions and single-copy sales (newsstand).
      a. Obtained generally by direct-mail promotion programs, and from subscription agency sales operations.

        Direct-mail programs promote potential subscribers on the following grounds: subscription copy cost is less than the newsstand cover price; the subscriber will receive all issues; home delivery is convenient; the magazine is received before it is available on the newsstand; and payment is not immediately required if there is a charge option.

        Subscription agencies receive a commission related to the costs of their sales operations. Some of the different types of agencies are:

        Catalog Agency. Publishes and mails catalogs to all types of libraries.

        Paid During Service (PDS) Agency. Subscriptions sold by field representatives to be paid for in monthly installments.

        Cash/Field, Paid in Advance (PIA), Agency. Subscriptions sold by field representative on a cash basis.

        School Plan Agency. Subscriptions sold by junior and senior high school students.

        Telephone Agency. Subscriptions and renewals sold using telephone marketing techniques.

        Department Store Agency. Suscription order forms included with store's invoice mailings to its own customers.

        Subcription agencies supplement the circulation department's own efforts to obtain subscribers and to maintain a predetermined circulation base.

b. Single Copy Sales (Newsstand). Permits an individual to purchase issues as desired, generally at the higher cover price.

A quantity based on various sales determinations is allocated to a national distributor. Wholesalers draw against this overall allocation for distribution to their retail outlets, e.g., newsstands, supermarkets, drug chains, transportation terminals, etc. Credit is allowed for unsold copies.

It is important, therefore, to distribute the right number of copies in the right place at the right time, and to assure that they are properly displayed.

III. GENERAL

1. Cost Per Issue. The publisher's cost for a single issue might be about 75 cents a copy, considering the costs of printing, paper, distribution, number of pages per issue, paper stock, inserts, etc. Accordingly, the publisher's cost for an annual subscription of 12 issues might be about $9.
2. Direct-Mail Promotion Cost. Depending on the contents of the promotion package, a mailing of 1,000 direct-mail pieces, including the art work, production, printing, paper, envelopes, order card, list rental, letterstop (inserting of material into the envelope), and postage, can be about $300 per 1,000. Assuming a 1 percent response factor, or 10 orders, the acquisition cost of each new subscription is $30.
3. Fulfillment Cost. The cost varies, depending upon the order entry needs (controlled coding, cash credit, credit card charge, gift, etc.) and type of fulfillment (to include caging, fulfillment, customer service, etc., or fulfillment only). The variation can be from about 35 cents to about $1.50 per name per year.
4. New Order Estimated Total Cost. Using the above, the estimated total annual cost (12 issues) would be $41, as follows:

$ 9.00	Cost of issues
30.00	Direct mail promotion
.80	Fulfillment (estimate)
1.20	Postage
$41.00	Total

5. Profit or Loss on an Acquired Subscription. Using the above, the acquisition profit or loss factor would relate, of course, to the price offered in promotion.

Renewals of subscriptions at the full price produce a profit.

Many circulation departments operate at a loss. The trend among the paid publications is to achieve at least a break-even level, and to sufficiently supplement the advertising revenue for continuing overall profitability.

6. Time, Deadlines, Schedules. These factors are vital to a circulation department's efficiency. Not meeting scheduled direct-mail drop dates, print-order due dates, invoice and renewal mail dates, etc., can seriously affect direct-mail response, invoice and renewal payment returns, etc., and create cash-flow problems.

IV.   FUNCTIONS

1. Process new and renewal orders, code for various needs and requirements, and enter.
2. Generate invoices for credit orders. Generate renewals in accordance with a predetermined renewal mailing program.
3. Apply credit payments.
4. Apply changes of address, nixies (undeliverables), etc. for updated file maintenance to produce scheduled issue, regional demographic, and supplementary label runs.
5. Produce required statistical data and financial reports.
6. Provide list rental runs in accordance with list selection requirements.

V.   CUSTOMER SERVICE

1. Acknowledge subscriber complaints, communicating with form letters and/or cards, personalized letters, or phone calls, as required.
2. Adjust complaints as required.
3. Mail missing issues.
4. Mail gift cards to gift subscription recipients.
5. Process refund requests, prorated to deduct for service ren-

dered, and adjust subscriber records accordingly. Each subscription is a contract to provide a specified service, and there is a liability until that service is completed.

VI. GENERAL

1. Fulfillment Cost. As mentioned earlier, cost per name per year varies, and is dependent upon processing, customer service, and publisher requirements.
2. Ordered-by-Mail Subscriptions. Orders received either from direct-mail campaigns or voluntary orders (white mail).
3. New Order. An order received for the first time. Subscriber has not been on file before.
4. Reinstated Order. An order received from a former subscriber who did not renew during period of service. Audit bureaus permit publishers to report subscriptions up to three months in arrears (grace copies) as paid subscriptions. For renewal and renewal percentage reporting, subscriptions can be considered renewals if the renewal is received within six months after expiration, and paid for within six months.
5. Renewal Order. A repeat order from the subscriber renewing the subscription, or renewing a subscription within six months after expiration.
6. Credit Orders vs. Paid Orders. A credit subscription is an implied promise to pay on receipt of invoice. Credit orders are entered with the required code information to receive invoices on a predetermined mailing program. Payments are applied as received to discontinue subsequent invoice mailings. A record is maintained of the number of credit copies served for deduction from paid circulation, and to be included in the unpaid distribution.

    Credit-card charge orders are more costly to process than paid orders.

    Paid orders include those received with the required payment, subscription agency orders, and credit-card charge orders.
7. Canadian and Foreign Orders. A credit option for domestic orders generally produces a higher return than a payment request. On Canadian and foreign orders a statement is generally added to the effect that payment is required in advance in U.S. funds, and includes a request for the additional post-

age. This procedure eliminates the additional processing and costs required for a credit order.

8. Group Subscription. Subscriptions in quantity sold to corporations, institutions, or individuals; addressed and mailed for employees, subsidiary companies, or branches; billed to the company at a reduced group rate.

9. Bulk Subscription. As defined by Business Publications Audit (BPA), two or more subscriptions to the same address; for Audit Bureau of Circulation (ABC) business publications, bulk subscription is five or more, and other magazines eleven or more to the same address, and generally at a lower bulk rate.

10. Special Billing. Other than a part of the regular computer-generated billing run. Most often required by institutions, schools, libraries, government agencies, etc.; to be typed to include special billing instructions, more than one copy, notarization, etc.

11. Subscriber Record Coding. Coding information required for circulation and audit needs, marketing, advertiser promotion, etc., is entered on a batch or code slip conforming to the publisher's coding layout, and is recorded with the order.

    Business publications require additional coding information for audit purposes, e.g., subscriber title or function, business and industry classification, qualification source, mailing address breakdown, and the optional audit reports. The required data can be a part of the subscription order and qualification form. Prompt classification and input permits immediate use of the data.

    Incorrect code input can, of course, produce erroneous audit, promotion, and marketing data, as well as subscriber complaints.

12. Match Code. Each order is entered with its individual computer-generated match code consisting of a combination of the name, address, and zip code. It appears as the first line of the address label. Match codes preclude duplicate order-entries. Also, the subscriber is quickly identified by the match code for the purposes of checking on complaints, etc.

13. Miscellaneous Order. Book club, record club, reprint, etc. orders are handled and processed separately from subscription orders. These miscellaneous orders can be coordinated by the circulation department, or, depending upon volume, by separate departments.

14. Non-Order Mail. Miscellaneous communications (white mail) other than orders, e.g., complaints, requests for information.

    Forms 3679 (nixies) received from the post office in brown envelopes for undeliverable copies are generally termed "brown" mail.

15. Processing of Non-Order Mail
    a. *Change of Address.* New address replaces address information in file.
    b. *Non-Paid Credit.* Discontinue service and maintain record of number of copies served for audit purposes.
    c. *Service Beyond Grace Period.* Discontinue service and maintain record of number of copies served beyond the three-issue-arrears grace period for audit purposes.
    d. *Post Office Undeliverables (Nixies).* It is advisable to contact the subscriber by first-class mail at the "undeliverable" address to either verify the address or to furnish a new address. In the meantime, discontinue service. If a confirming reply is received, reinstate the subscription and extend for the number of missing issues.
    e. *Duplicate Paid Order.* Either combine the duplicate paid order with the existing paid subscription and extend the subscription or refund the duplicate payment based on the publisher's policy.
    f. *Late Delivery.* Determine from the subscriber's record that the issue was mailed on schedule. Advise subscriber accordingly, indicating the approximate post-office delivery time, and suggesting that the subscriber contact the local postmaster regarding a possible delivery problem.

16. Promotions. Subscription promotions often offer a premium, a lower price, or a longer term to potential new and/or charter subscribers to induce a higher response. Should an active subscriber inadvertently receive any of the promotions and request the benefit, it is generally advisable (to solidify customer goodwill) to promptly acknowledge and mail the offered premium, and/or adjust the subscriber's account accordingly. Then file the document with the original order for audit justification.

17. Cancellation and Refund Requests. Requests for service terminations and refunds can come in during the life of the subscription, upon receipt of the invoice, or upon receipt of the renewal reminder. To save the subscription, it may be

advisable to first contact the subscriber in an attempt to resell the subscription. Should that fail, process the requested termination and issue a refund prorated as required.

18. Computerization of Fulfillment Services
    a. More and more fulfillment and circulation operations are being automated. Computerization reduces manual detail.
    b. Computer fulfillment systems accept and store for retrieval enormous amounts of information, generate required output speedily and effectively, and provide for growth through all their capabilities.
    c. Equipment (hardware), programs (software), and technical operating personnel are high-cost factors to be considered in connection with the feasibility of an in-house operation.
    d. Equipment can be either leased or purchased. The economics of both should be considered. Since computer manufacturers are continually improving their equipment and introducing new models, buying equipment may restrict a purchaser indefinitely to less-efficient equipment.
    e. Outside Fulfillment Services. Many publishers, including the multi-magazine publishers, have found that using the services of a specialized fulfillment service is more advantageous than attempting to perform their own fulfillment services. The publisher has the full use of the service bureau's equipment, operations, and personnel, but is only paying a small part of the overall costs.

19. Criteria for Selecting a Service Bureau
    a. Number of years in business.
    b. Number of accounts and reputation of the accounts.
    c. Type and capability of operational equipment and personnel.
    d. Control of the equipment.
    e. Industry recognition and reputation.

20. Publisher's Fulfillment Requirements. Depending upon the publisher's own operations and needs, service bureaus provide either partial or full service.
    a. *Partial Service.* The service bureau provides all the required computer operations and related personnel, excluding the front-end or clerical operations and caging (coding of documents).
    b. *Full Service.* In addition to the computer operations, the service bureau handles all the clerical, caging, customer-

service, and related operations, such as letterstop, printing, and mailing.

AUDIT BUREAUS (BPA and ABC)

I.   OBJECTIVES. To issue standardized statements of circulation data and related data, verify a publisher's figures by audit of required records, and disseminate data for the benefit of advertisers, advertising agencies, and others. Such data provide measurement standards for advertising considerations.

II. TYPES OF BUREAUS. There are two major audit service bureaus, both independent, tripartite organizations of publishers, advertisers, and advertising agencies.

1. BPA (Business Publications Audit of Circulation, Inc.). Primarily audits business publications.
2. ABC (Audit Bureau of Circulations). Audits business publications, farm publications, consumer publications, and newspapers.

Both organizations have excellent reputations. The choice of an audit bureau generally is related to the publication's market and type of circulation.

III. TYPES OF CIRCULATION REPORTS. For each 6-month period, a 6-month publisher's statement is filed with the audit bureau. The two 6-month publisher's statements are then audited and consolidated into a 12-month audit report.

Both organizations also provide optional special marketing services, i.e., Unit Audit Report, Supplementary Audit Report, Census Audit Report, Optional Addenda Audit Report, Duplication Audit Report, and Pass-Along Audit Report.

IV. ADDITIONAL CIRCULATION INFORMATION SOURCES. Advertisers and advertising agencies often refer to SRDS (Standard Rate & Data Service, Inc.), a reference book containing listings of publishers who accept advertising, and including information on the publication's audience, production requirements, advertising rates, circulation figures, etc.

Other sources include reader demographic and product usage studies, plus special reports, generally undertaken by a research firm selected by the publisher.

V.   STATEMENT PARAGRAPHS. The publisher's statement for business publications of both audit organizations includes the following paragraphs for completion:

ABC	BPA
Paragraph:	Paragraph:
(1a) Average paid circulation for the period reported.	(1) Average qualified circulation breakdown for the period reported. Average nonqualified distribution.
(1b) Average non-paid distribution to the field service for the period reported.	
(2) Paid circulation and non-paid distribution to field served by issues, and non-paid removals and additions.	(2) Qualified circulation by issue, with removals and additions for the period reported.
(3) Business analysis of total paid subscription of circulation for the May or November issue.	(3a) Business/occupational breakdown of qualified circulation for the May or November issue.
	(3b) Qualification source breakdown for the May or November issue.
	(3c) Mailing address breakdown of qualified circulation for the May or November issue.
(4) Geographic analysis for the May or November issue.	(4) Geographic breakdown of qualified circulation for the May or November issue.
(5) Authorized prices and total subscriptions sold for the period reported.	(5) Prices.
(6) Duration of subcriptions sold.	(6) Sources.

ABC		BPA	
(7)	Channels of subcription sales.	(7)	Premiums.
(8)	Use of premiums.	(8)	Length of subscriptions.
(9)	Arrears and extensions.	(9)	Status of qualified paid subscription payments for the May or November issue.
(10)	Renewals of paid subscriptions.	(10)	Renewal percentage of qualified paid circulation.
(11)	Explanatory (to amplify or explain data).	(11)	Additional data.

VI.   GENERAL

1. *Basic Price.* Regular price at which the publication may be purchased. This price appears in the identification statement.
2. *Lower Than Basic Price.* Reduction from the basic price to promote new subscriptions; also, to induce renewals.
3. *Premiums.* A circulation sales incentive, such as an atlas or a book, to promote new subscriptions; also, to induce renewals. The use and value of premiums are regulated by the audit organizations.

VII.   CRITERIA FOR ANALYZING THE STATEMENT REPORTING OF NEW AND RENEWAL SUBSCRIPTIONS (by paragraph number in Section V, above).

ABC		BPA	
Paragraph (5)	Authorized prices.	Paragraph (5)	Prices.
Paragraph (6)	Duration of subscription.	Paragraph (6)	Sources.
Paragraph (7)	Channels of subscription sales.	Paragraph (7)	Premiums.
Paragraph (8)	Use of premiums.	Paragraph (8)	Length of subscriptions.

VIII.   RENEWAL REPORTING. Paragraph 10 (as in Section V, above) establishes the percentage of subscription renewals for a given period. This information serves as a guideline to determine edi-

torial effectiveness. Advertisers and advertising agencies analyze the degree of interest by the numbers and percentages of subscribers who renew their subscriptions.

MARKETING—SUBSCRIPTIONS, etc.

There are a number of areas that can be developed into profit centers to obtain a more profitable circulation operation overall. Several are listed below.

List Rentals. Renting active and expired subscriber lists for a one-time rental use at a predetermined "per 1,000" names price. Rental and billing details can be handled by the circulation department, or by a list management service, charging 10 percent of the list rental rate.

Book Club. Offering books of interest to the publication's subscribers and readers on either a negative or positive option plan.

Merchandise Club. Offering products of interest to the publication's subscribers and readers through the publication's own pages, flyers, billing and renewal inserts, catalogs, etc.

Back Issues. Offering available back issues through house ads, at a price that includes both postage and handling.

Library Case or Binder. Advising subscribers through house ads, billing, and renewal inserts, etc., of the availability of library cases and binders to permanently store issues. Manufacture and shipping are handled by an outside source, with a commission to the publisher for each case or binder sold.

Reprints. Announcing through house ads that reprints of articles, features, etc. are available, and at quantity discount prices.

Directories. Developing a directory of sources, buying information, etc.; updated annually.

Newsletters. Spinning off popular features into newsletters.

Other profit centers can also be developed, consistent with the type of publication and its audience.

Marketing has been summarized as reaching the right people at the right time with the right product at the right price. This philosophy can lend itself to new subscription promotion programs, renewal programs, telephone promotions, and advertising space sales programs.

I.   NEW SUBSCRIPTION PROMOTION. Following are some marketing programs to consider for new subscription promotion.

1. Direct Mail. Most commonly used program for soliciting new subscription orders. Depending upon the components of the promotion package, the cost can be $300 per 1,000 and up. A return of 1 to 2 percent is generally considered successful.

   It is desirable to test different mailing periods to determine which is most effective for a particular publication. Some surveys indicate that January is most productive and June least productive.

   "Bill me" and credit-card charge options increase the response factor.

   The recent introduction of ink-jet printers, which spray ink on a page in the shape of a character, eliminates the need to affix labels. Also, these high-quality printing devices are suitable for creating personalized letters. Advertisers generally consider subscriptions obtained through direct mail to be a highly desirable part of the circulation mix.

2. Bind-In and Blow-In Cards. Single and double bind-in cards are bound into each issue to promote new subscriptions, gift subscriptions, renewals, or any combination of these. Blow-in cards, inserted as the term indicates, are used similarly. Studies have shown that blow-in cards pull better response than do bind-in cards.

3. House Ads. House ads permitting a coupon can also be considered for promotions.

4. New Name Recommendations. Request subscribers to furnish names and addresses of friends who would also be interested in receiving the publication; offer the subscriber a premium for sending along the requested number of names.

   This promotion can also be included in the direct mail package for new subscription solicitations, offering the potential subscriber a premium for sending along the requested number of names and addresses.

5. Lifetime Subscriptions. A lifetime subscription offer can be considered in connection with new subscription promotions for cash-flow purposes; lifetime subscriptions also eliminate costs of renewal mailings. But do consider the probable effects of inflation on the costs of servicing a lifetime subscriber.

6. Co-Op Mailings. Various types of co-op mailings include stuffers with department store mailings, a loose or bound per-

forated card included with other mailers, etc. Participants share all costs.

7. PI (Per Inquiry). A commission on a "per inquiry" response basis is established with the participant in the promotion.

8. Fund Raising. Arrange with civic and community organizations, fraternal organizations, clubs, etc., to sell subscriptions on the basis of a commission for each sale.

9. Reader Service Cards. Generally applicable to trade and business publications. Specific reader service numbers are assigned to ads, new product information, manufacturer's literature, etc. Reader service cards (commonly known as "bingo cards") containing all the numbers are bound into the publication; readers may request specific information by circling the appropriate numbers. Bingo cards are generally valid for three months. These cards often include provisions for new subscription solicitation, renewal requests, and additional name references for promotion.

10. Retail Program. Arrangements are made with retail outlets related to the publication's readership to sell on a commission basis or distribute the publication. Racks, window decals, display stands, and other promotional material are provided the retail store.

11. Expires. It can prove profitable to promote expirations after six-month expiration periods to induce former subscribers to resubscribe. Promotions could highlight what subscribers missed, as well as forthcoming features. A reduced promotion price could be considered.

12. Trade-Outs. Page space and bind-in cards are exchanged with other publications on a space or circulation-count basis. Trades should be considered consistent with the potential interest of the trading publication's readers.

II.   RENEWAL. Extend the subscription at a fraction of the cost of originally obtaining it.

III.   TELEPHONE. The telephone has become an important tool in marketing. An "800" toll-free, 24-hour, 7-day service number is usually included in all promotions and promotional material.
       Some of the uses of the telephone are:
       a. Soliciting new subscriptions and selling longer terms.

     b. Soliciting renewals toward the end of a renewal series.
     c. Contacting dropped expirations to encourage resub-
        scriptions.
     d. Pretesting lists for market-profile data before going into
        the mail.
     e. Promoting Christmas and other anniversary subscription
        promotions.

Charge-card options help to induce additional order responses.

Invoices with thank-you acknowledgments should go out the same day the order is sold. Subscriptions should be started immediately.

IV.   ADVERTISING SPACE SALES. Advertisers are interested in reaching an audience—at a favorable cost per 1,000 circulation—that is actively interested in buying their products or services.

    Following are some marketing factors of interest to advertisers in determining their advertising schedule:

1. Demographic (measurable externals of life patterns, i.e., age, income, education, occupation, etc.) and psychographic (emotional and lifestyle buying trends) data.
2. Reader product-buying habits.
3. Regional and demographic editions to reach a specific audience.
4. Merchandising support, e.g., mounting the advertiser's ad for display purposes for the advertiser's sales outlets.

    The publisher should research current census data in order to know as much as possible about a publication's audience, as well as to obtain data to encourage advertising sales.

FEDERAL TRADE COMMISSION (FTC) REGULATIONS

FTC regulations cover many potential problem areas relating to mail-order shipping. For example:

    If merchandise cannot be shipped within the time stated in the ad, or within 30 days if no time is specified, the consumer must be notified of the delay, with an indication of the revised shipment date, and given the option of cancelling the order.

    The consumer must be furnished a postage-free "device" to reply.

    If the consumer so indicates, the order must be cancelled.

If the consumer does not respond to the delay notice, it can be presumed that consent has been granted for a 30-day delay period from the original promised delivery date.

For delays beyond this extended period, the consumer must actively consent, or the payment must be refunded.

These rules do not cover every mail-order product or service. For example, they do not cover magazine subscriptions or other serial deliveries—except for the first issue, which is covered.

POST OFFICE REQUIREMENTS

1. ZIP CODES (5 digits). The zip code system is based on a series of standard geographic units. The United States is divided into ten large areas; each area is given a number between 0 to 9, the first digit of the zip code. Key post offices in each area are designated sectional centers, the next two digits. Each sectional center serves a series of associated post offices, the last two digits.

    Zip codes are required for all second- and third-class bulk mailings, as well as for the presort saving for first-class and second- and third-class bulk mailings.

    a. A new "Zip for Ships" delivery service has been introduced for U.S. Navy destinations that previously went only to the FPO zip codes in New York, San Francisco, and Seattle. The program introduces 188 unique codes for vessels with crews of 750 or more stationed around the world.

    b. The U.S. Postal Service is planning to implement an expanded nine-digit zip code to enable it to partially automate the secondary incoming sortation into small-delivery segments for carriers. The extra four digits will be linked to the five digits by a hyphen. The Postal Service will make available computer tapes for its data base.

2. CANADIAN POSTAL CODE (6 digits). Mail addressed to Canada should include the Canadian Postal Code. (*The Canadian Postal Standards & Code Guide* can be obtained from Marketing, Canada Post, Confederation Heights, Ottawa, Ontario K1A0Y2.)

3. PRESORTED MAIL

    a. Presorted first-class mail offers mailers a two-cent reduced postage rate for letters, and a reduced one-cent postage rate for postcards sorted by zip code, and meeting other postal requirements.

    b. Presorted third-class bulk mail offers mailers a savings ranging from 8.4 cents per piece to 6 or 7 cents per piece sorted by zip code, and meeting other postal requirements.

c. The Postal Service is offering a national scheme computer tape containing the city carrier route, rural route, star route, lockbox schemes for use in presort second-class mail, and carrier route presorted third-class mail.

4. PAID AND REQUEST CIRCULATION. Controlled circulation is no longer a separate postal classification, and all periodicals, both paid and controlled/request (that meet basic entry requirements), use the second-class postal rate.

The second-class postal rate consists of a per-piece charge (to which presort discounts apply); an editorial pound rate that does not increase with distance; and a pound charge that varies according to distance, applied to the advertising content. Former controlled circulation periodicals (now called Second Class Alternative II) pay the same rate as Second Class Alternative I periodicals (paid circulation periodicals). Both are second-class periodicals. Publications that do not meet either the Second Class Alternative I or II requirements would use the third-class rate.

There are also basic requirements for Second Class Alternative II periodicals, which are:

- Fifty percent or more of the recipients must request the periodical (contrasted to Alternative I, in which 50 percent of the recipients must pay for the periodical).
- There must be 25 percent editorial content in every issue (as opposed to an average of 25 percent over a 12-month period for Alternative I periodicals).
- There must be independent ownership (no house organs can use the Alternative II).
- The periodical must be published at least four times a year (Alternative I periodicals also have this requirement).
- The periodical must contain at least 24 pages per issue (Alternative I periodicals do not have this requirement).

Alternative II periodicals can have a combination of paid subscriptions and direct requests in order to comply with the 50-percent request requirement. The Postal Service intends to work closely with both the ABC and the BPA in order to verify whether or not Alternative II periodicals meet the 50-percent request requirement. The ABC and the PBC already do this for Alternative I periodicals when the Postal Service wants to verify the paid subscriber list.

5. ALTERNATIVE DELIVERY. Delivery service by private carriers for other than first-class mail, generally for paid publications.

Private carriers cannot deposit magazines in a mailbox or chute used by the Postal Service for delivery of mail. The magazine has to be placed on a doorknob, on the doorstep, or in a special receptacle reserved for it.

The private carriers generally do not have access to high- security apartment houses. Alternative delivery is essentially for the large circulation magazines with high distribution in the metropolitan areas.

Users of alternative delivery have found that the private carriers provide more economical and faster home delivery than that presently available from the Postal Service. However, the additional costs of shipping the magazines from the printer to the private carrier should be considered.

6. DUPLICATE FORMS 3579. It is not unusual to receive multiple Forms 3579 from the Postal Service for undeliverable copies. The duplicates should be returned with the appropriate completed post office form for a refund of the duplicate payments.

7. PUBLICATION IDENTIFICATION NUMBER. Either the U.S. Postal Service or ISSN (International Standard Serial Number, administered by the Library of Congress) publication number is required in a publication's publisher identification paragraph, to immediately follow the name of the publication.

8. CITY AND STATE ABBREVIATIONS. The Postal Service provides standard two-letter abbreviations for all states, as well as standard abbreviations for cities with long names.

9. STANDARD MAIL PIECES. The Postal Service has implemented size standards for envelopes, cards, and other pieces of mail capable of being machine sorted to compensate for added costs of handling items that must be manually sorted.

The limitations apply only to first-class mail and airmail weighing one ounce or less, and single-piece third-class mail weighing two ounces or less and more than 6 1/8 inches high or 11 1/2 inches long or 1/4 inch thick; also, to pieces with a length that is less than 1.3 times the height or more than 2.5 times the height, and less than .007 inches thick.

Mail pieces exceeding these limits will be declared "nonstandard" and subject to a surcharge in addition to the applicable postage and fees.

10. FACING IDENTIFICATION MARK (FIM). The FIM is a bar code

pattern that functions as an orientation mark for the Postal Service's automatic facing and cancelling equipment.

It is required on all Business Reply Cards and Business Reply Envelopes (up to 6 1/8 inches X 11 1/2 inches), and must appear along the top edge and to the left of the NO POSTAGE endorsement.

11. POSTAL SERVICE AUDITS. Publishers can be relieved of direct Postal Service audits of their circulation as a result of agreements reached with the Audit Bureau of Circulations, Inc. (ABC) and the Business Publications Audit of Circulation (BPA). Participation is optional. The agreement provides that the Postal Service will accept the audit reports and other related data as the annual verification of circulation for the Statement of Mailing—Second Class Publications and Statement of Ownership, Management, and Circulation required by the Postal Service for publications entered as second-class.

12. WRAPPER ADVERTISING. A new section has been added to the *Postal Service Manual* permitting publishers to print advertising and other material on wrappers, sleeves, and envelopes in which second-class publications are enclosed.

The appropriate second-class rate for advertising matter will be charged for the printed advertising. The advertising is to be included in calculating the amount of advertising for the issue.

13. ENCLOSURES FOR CONTROLLED PUBLICATIONS. Controlled publications may have enclosures, such as receipts and orders for subscriptions, as similarly allowed for regular rate second-class publications. These may be inserted loose or bound into the publication.

The preparation methods include, but are not limited to: Printed or hand written; printed on cards and envelopes, including business reply cards; arranged to include coin receptacles; or arranged as combination forms for two or more controlled circulation or second-class publications issued by the same publisher.

14. QUALIFYING BACK ISSUES OF CONTROLLED CIRCULATION COPIES. Qualifying copies of back issues of controlled circulation publications are now permitted to be mailed at the controlled rates of postage. Back issues and reprints of the following publications meeting the requirements outlined in Section 521 of the *Domestic Mail Manual* may be mailed at the controlled circulation rates.

a. Unbound copies of back issues, as long as the publication's controlled circulation entry is in effect.

b. Unbound reprint copies of daily publications printed within one week of the date of issue.
c. Unbound reprint copies of other than daily publications, printed before the next issue is printed.
d. Other reprints and bound back issues are charged with postage at the applicable third- or fourth-class rates.

Colleges and Universities Offering Courses in Business Journalism

The number of schools or departments of journalism offering specific courses in business journalism is increasing each year. It is likely that before the year 2000 nearly every major school or department of journalism will have a business journalism program or course. Following is the current listing.

The American University
School of Communication
Massachusetts & Nebraska Aves.,
  NW
Washington, DC 20016
(202) 686-2055

Laird B. Anderson, Director
Graduate Program in Journalism
  & Public Affairs

California State University
Department of Communications
Fullerton, CA 91634
(714) 773-3517

Carolyn Johnson, Acting Chair

University of California
School of Journalism
Berkeley, CA 94720
(415) 642-3383

Edwin R. Bayley, Dean

Colorado State University
Department of Technical
  Journalism
Fort Collins, CO 80523
(303) 491-6310

Derry Eynon, Acting Chairman

Columbia University
New York, NY 10027
(212) 280-3571

Osborn Elliott, Dean

University of Georgia
School of Journalism and
  Mass Communication
Athens, GA 30602
(404) 542-4668

Scott M. Cutlip, Dean

Northern Illinois University
Department of Journalism
DeKalb, IL 60115
(815) 753-1925

Irvan J. Kummerfeldt, Chairman

Iowa State University
Department of Journalism and
  Mass Communication
Ames, IA 50011
(515) 294-4340

J. K. Hvistendahl, Chairman

The University of Iowa
School of Journalism and Mass
  Communication
Iowa City, IA 52242
(319) 353-5414

Kenneth Starck, Director

Michigan State University
School of Journalism
East Lansing, MI 48824
(517) 355-3410

Elizabeth Yamashita, Chair

University of Missouri
School of Journalism
Columbia, MO 65211
(314) 882-7862

James K. Gentry, Director
Business Journalism Program

University of Nebraska
School of Journalism
Lincoln, NE 68588
(402) 472-3044

Neale Copple, Dean
School of Journalism

New York University
Gallatin Division
715 Broadway
New York, NY 10003
(212) 598-7077

Herbert I. London, Dean*

Northwestern University
The Medill School of Journalism
Evanston, IL 60201
(312) 492-7371

I. W. Cole, Dean

Ohio University
School of Journalism
Athens OH 45701
(614) 594-5013

Cortland Anderson, Director

Oklahoma State University
School of Journalism and
  Broadcasting
Stillwater, OK 74078
(405) 624-6354

Marlan Nelson, Interim Director

Oregon State University
Department of Journalism
Eugene, OR 97403
(503) 686-3738

Roy Halverson, Associate Professor

Temple University
School of Communications and
  Theater
Philadelphia, PA 19122
(215) 787-7433

University of Tennessee
College of Communications
Knoxville, TN 37916
(615) 974-3031

Donald G. Hileman, Dean

North Texas State University
Department of Journalism
Denton, TX 76203
(817) 921-7425

Reg Westmoreland, Chairman

*A special program of business journalism has been developed at the Gallatin Division of New York University, including a selection of courses in the Department of Journalism together with courses in the School of Business and the School of Arts and Sciences.

Publishers of Multiple Business Publications

Following is a selected listing of companies publishing multiple business publications. For a more comprehensive list check the membership of the American Business Press, Inc., and the Multiple Business Publication Publishers Index in the *Business Publication Rates and Data*, published monthly by Standard Rate & Data Service, Inc.

Ashlee Publishing Company, Inc.
110 E. 42 St.
New York, NY 10017
(212) 682-7681

Oscar S. Glasberg, Vice President

Bill Communications, Inc.
633 Third Avenue
New York, NY 10017
(212) 986-4800

Morgan T. Browne, President

Billboard Publications, Inc.
1515 Broadway
New York, NY 10036
(212) 764-7300

William D. Littleford, Chairman

BMT Publications, Inc.
254 W. 31 St.
New York, NY 10001
(212) 594-4120

Irwin Breitman, President

Brentwood Publishing Corp.
825 S. Barrington Avenue
Los Angeles, CA 90049
(213) 826-8388

Martin W. Waldman, President

Cahners Publishing Co.
221 Columbus Avenue
Boston, MA 02116
(617) 536-7780

Saul Goldweitz, President

Chilton Co.
Chilton Way
Radnor, PA 19089
(215) 964-4000

Lawrence A. Fornasieri, President

Columbia Communications, Inc.
370 Lexington Avenue
New York, NY 10017
(212) 532-9290

Joseph D. Feldman, President

Communications Channels, Inc.
Subsidiary, Argus Press
Holding, Ltd.,
London, England
6285 Barfield Road
Atlanta, GA 30328
(404) 256-9800

Benjamin Kotscher, President

Crain Communications, Inc.
740 N. Rush St.
Chicago, IL 60622
(312) 649-5200

Rance Crain, President

CW Communications, Inc.
375 Cochituate Road, Box 880
Framingham, MA 01701
(617) 879-0700

Patrick McGovern, Chairman

Davies Publishing Co.
136 Shore Drive
Hinsdale, IL 60521
(312) 325-2930

Robert E. Davies, President

Ebel-Doctorow Publications, Inc.
1115 Clifton Avenue
Clifton, NJ 07013
(201) 779-1600

Donald Doctorow, President

Fairchild Publications, Inc.
7 E. 12 St.
New York, NY 10003
(212) 741-4000

John B. Sias, President

Folio Magazine Publishing Corp.
125 Elm St., P.O. Box 697
New Canaan, CT 06840
(203) 972-0761

Joseph J. Hanson, President

Geyer-McAllister Publications, Inc.
51 Madison Avenue
New York, NY 10010
(212) 689-4411

Donald McAllister, Chairman

Gordon Publications, Inc.
20 Community Place, CN 1952
Morristown, NJ 07960
(201) 267-6040

Theodore Gordon, Chairman

Gorman Publishing Co.
5725 East River Road
Chicago, IL 60631
(312) 693-3200

William L. Gorman, President

Gralla Publications
1515 Broadway
New York, NY 10036
(212) 869-1300

Lawrence Gralla, President

Gulf Publishing Co.
3301 Allen Parkway
Houston, TX 77019
(713) 529-4301

William G. Dudley, President

Hayden Publishing Co., Inc.
10 Mulholland Drive
Hasbrouck Heights, NJ 07604
(201) 393-6000

James S. Mulholland, Jr.,
  President

HBJ Communications and
  Services, Inc.
Harcourt Brace Jovanovich, Inc.
757 Third Avenue
New York, NY 10017
(212) 888-3100

Robert L. Edgell, Chairman

Hearst Business Communications,
Inc.
645 Stewart Avenue
Garden City, NY 11530
(516) 222-2500
Robert J. Males, President

Hitchcock Publishing Co.
Hitchcock Building
Wheaton, IL 60187
(213) 665-1000
Loren M. Walsh, President

Hoffman Publications
3000 NE 30th Pl., P.O. Box 11299
Ft. Lauderdale, FL 33306
(305) 566-8401

The Hollywood Reporter, Inc.
6715 Sunset Boulevard
Hollywood, CA 90028
(213) 464-7411
Tichi Wilkerson, Publisher

Industry Media, Inc.
1129 E. 17th Avenue
Denver, CO 80218
(303) 832-1022
Charles Cleworth, President

International Thomson Business
Press
Two Radnor Corporate Center
P.O. Box 301
Radnor, PA 19087
(215) 687-9607
Richard H. Groves, President

Intertec Publishing Corp.
9221 Quivira Road
Overland Park, KS 66215
(913) 888-4664
R. J. Hancock, President

Irving-Cloud Publishing Co., Inc.
7300 N. Cicero
Chicago, IL 60646
(213) 588-7300
Taylor L. Kennedy, President

Jobson Publishing Corp.
488 Madion Avenue
New York, NY 10022
(212) 758-5620
Robert Amato, President

Johnson Hill Press, Inc.
1233 Janesville Avenue
Fort Atkinson, WI 53538
(414) 563-6388
Jonathan Pellegrin, President

Lakewood Publications, Inc.
731 Hennepin Avenue
Minneapolis, MN 55403
(612) 333-0471
Thomas J. Nammacher, Chairman

Lebhar-Friedman, Inc.
425 Park Avenue
New York, NY 10022
(212) 371-9400
J. Roger Friedman, President

Maclean Hunter Publishing Corp.
300 West Adams St.
Chicago, IL 60606
(213) 726-2802
Joseph J. O'Neill, President

McGraw-Hill Publications Co.
1221 Avenue of the Americas
New York, NY 10021
(212) 997-1221
John G. Wrede, President

McKnight Medical Communications, Inc.
500 Frontage Road
Northfield, IL 60093
(312) 446-1622
William M. McKnight, President

Miller Freeman Publications, Inc.
500 Howard St.
San Francisco, CA 94105
(415) 397-1881
Marshall W. Freeman, President

The Miller Publishing Co.
2501 Wayzata Boulevard
Minneapolis, MN 55440
(612) 374-5200
Richard C. Marshall, President

Morgan-Grampian Publishing Co.
2 Park Avenue
New York, NY 10016
(212) 340-9700
Ronald Evans, President

National Underwriter Co.
420 E. Fourth St.
Cincinnati, OH 45202
(513) 721-2140
John Z. Hershede, Chairman

North American Publishing Co.
401 N. Broad St.
Philadelphia, PA 19108
(225) 574-9600
I. J. Borowsky, President

Office Publications, Inc.
1200 Summer St.
Stamford, CT 06901
(203) 327-9670
William Schulhof, Editor

Pennwell Publishing Co.
1421 S. Sheridan Rd.
Tulsa, OK 74112
(918) 835-3161
Philip C. Lauinger, Jr., President

Penton/IPC, Inc.
1111 Chester Avenue
Cleveland, OH 44144
(216) 696-7000
Sal F. Marino, President

Pergamon Press, Inc.
Maxwell House, Fairview Park
Elmsford, NY 10523
(914) 592-7700
Richard C. Rowson, President

PTN Publishing Corp.
250 Fulton Avenue
Hempstead, NJ 11550
(516) 489-1300
Rudolf Maschke, Publisher

Putman Publishing Co.
301 E. Erie St.
Chicago, IL 60611
(312) 644-2020
Grace Cappelleti, President

Schnell Publishing Co., Inc.
100 Church St.
New York, NY 10007
(212) 732-9820
Arthur R. Kavaler, President

Scranton Gillette Communications, Inc.
380 Northwest Highway
Des Plaines, IL 60616
(213) 694-2410
E. Scranton Gillette, Chairman

Simmons-Boardman Publishing
  Corp.
345 Hudson St.
New York, NY 10014
(212) 620-7200
Arthur J. McGinnis, Chairman

Smith, W. R. C., Publishing Co.
1760 Peachtree Rd., NW
Atlanta, GA 30309
(404) 874-4462
Walter Mitchell, Jr., President

Sosland Publishing Co.
4800 Main St.
Kansas City, MO 64112
(816) 756-1000
Morton I. Sosland, President

ST Publications
407 Gilbert Avenue
Cincinnati, OH 45202
(513) 421-2050
Dave R. Swormstedt, Jr., President

Standard Rate & Data Service, Inc.
(subsidiary of Macmillan, Inc.)
5201 Old Orchard Road
Skokie, IL 60077
(312) 470-3100
Dale R. Bauer, President

Technical Publishing Co.
666 Fifth Avenue
New York, NY 10103
(212) 489-2200
J. K. Abley, Chairman

Technical Reporting Corp.
1098 S. Milwaukee Avenue
P.O. Box 745
Wheeling, IL 60090
(312) 537-6460
Earl Palmer, President

Thomas Publishing Co.
One Penn Plaza
New York, NY 10119
(212) 695-0500
Carl T. Holst-Knudsen, President

United Business Publications, Inc.
(subsidiary of Media Horizons,
  Inc.)
475 Park Avenue South
New York, NY 10016
(212) 725-2300
Joel Harnett, President

Vance Publishing Corp.
300 West Adams St.
Chicago, IL 60606
(312) 977-7200
John B. O'Neil, President

Watt Publishing Co.
Sandstone Building
Mount Morris, IL 61054
(815) 734-4171
Leslie A. Watt, President

Whitney Communications Corp.
Magazine Division
850 Third Avenue
New York, NY 10022
(212) 593-2100
John S. Prescott, President

Ziff-Davis Publishing Co.
One Park Avenue
New York, NY 10016
(212) 725-3500
Philip Sine, Sr. Vice President

CANADA

Canadian Engineering Publications Ltd.
32 Front St., W
Toronto, Ont. M5J 2H9, Canada
(416) 869-1735

Charles F. Broad, President

Clifford/Elliot & Assoc. Ltd.
1289 Marlborough Ct.
Oakville, Ont. L6H 2R9, Canada
(416) 842-2884

Maclean Hunter Business Publishing Co.
481 University Avenue
Toronto, Ont. M5W 1A7, Canada
(416) 596-5000

Robert W. Robertson,
Vice President

Page Publications Ltd.
380 Wellington St., W
Toronto, Ont. M5V 1E3, Canada
(416) 366-4608

Gwendolyn Page, President

Southan Communications Ltd.
1450 Don Mills Road
Don Mills, Ont. M3B 2X7, Canada
(416) 445-6641

E. J. Mannion, Chairman

Whitsed Publishing Ltd.
55 Bloor St., W.
Toronto, Ont. M4W 3M1, Canada
(416) 967-6200

Roy J. Whitsed, President/Publisher

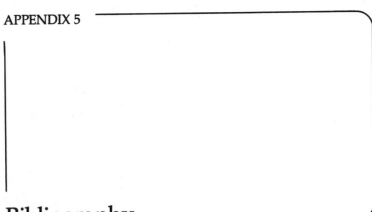

Bibliography

Bell, D., et al. *Writing for Fortune: Nineteen Authors Remember Life on the Staff of a Remarkable Magazine*. New York: Time, Inc., 1980. 194 pp.

Bethell, T. *The Television Evening News Covers Inflation 1978-79*. Media Institute, 1980. 52 pp.

Burlingame, R. *Endless Frontiers: The Story of McGraw-Hill*. New York: McGraw-Hill Book Co., 1959. 506 pp.

Crain Communications, Inc. *Fifty Years of Marketing and the Business Press*. Chicago: Crain Communications, Inc., 1966. 244 pp. (*Industrial Marketing*'s 50th anniversary issue.)

Dodds, R. H. *Writing for Technical and Business Magazines*. New York: John Wiley & Sons, 1969. 194 pp.

Du Vall, D. F. *Grab Your Share of the Wealth*. Williamston, Mich.: Du Vall Press Financial Publications, 1978.

Elfenbein, J. *Business Journalism*. 1960. Reprint. Westport, Conn.: Greenwood Press.

———. *Business Publishing Practice*. 1952. Reprint. Westport, Conn.: Greenwood Press, 1970. 422 pp.

Finn, D. *The Business-Media Relationship: Countering Misconceptions and Distrust*. New York: AMACOM, 1981. 92 pp. (Based on a study conducted by Research & Forecasts, Inc., in cooperation with the American Management Associates.)

Folio Magazine Publishing Corp. *Magazine Publishing Management*. New Canaan, Conn.: Folio Magazine Publishing Corp., 1976. 299 pp.

Ford, J. L. *Magazines for Millions—The Story of Specialized Publications*. Carbondale, Ill.: Southern Illinois University Press., 1969. 320 pp.

Freeman, E. L. *Independence in All Things. Neutrality in Nothing*. San Francisco: Miller Freeman Publications, 1973. 255 pp. (The story of Leigh Richmond Freeman, pioneer journalist.)

Gussow, D. *Divorce Corporate Style*. New York: Ballantine Books, 1972. 403 pp. (The story of the sale of Magazines For Industry, Inc., to Cowles Communications, Inc., in 1966, and its buy back by Don Gussow and his associates in 1970.)

Harwell, G. C. *Technical Communication*. New York: Macmillan Publishing Co., 1960. 392 pp.

Hays, R. *Principles of Technical Writing*. Reading, Mass: Addison-Wesley Publishing Co., 1965. 318 pp.

Hofsoos, E. *What Management Should Know About Industrial Advertising*. Houston: Gulf Publishing Co., 1970. 318 pp.

Kirsch, D. *Documentary Supplement to Financial and Economic Journalism: Analysis, Interpretation, and Reporting*. New York: New York University Press, 1978.

———. *Financial and Economic Journalism: Analysis, Interpretation, and Reporting*. New York: New York University Press, 1978.

Kohlmeier, L. M., et al., ed. *Reporting on Business and the Economy*. Englewood Cliffs, N.J.: Prentice-Hall, Inc., 1981. 336 pp.

Lewis, J. E. *Who Are Those Guys?: A Monograph for Business on the News Media Today*. Washington, D.C.: The Media Institute, 1981. 26 pp.

MacDougall, A. K. *Ninety Seconds to Tell It All: Big Business and the News Media*. Homewood, Ill.: Dow-Jones-Irwin, 1981. 250 pp.

McGuire, D. *Technical and Industrial Journalism*. Harrisburg, Penn.: Stackpole Books, 1956. 184 pp.

McPhatter, W., ed. *The Business Beat: Its Impact and Its Problems*. Bobbs Merrill, 1980. 168 pp.

Marder, D. *The Craft of Technical Writing*. New York: Macmillan Publishing Co., 1960. 392 pp.

Messner, F. R. *Industrial Advertising—Planning, Creating, Evaluating and Merchandising It More Effectively*. New York: McGraw-Hill Book Co., 1963. 314 pp.

Myers, K. H., Jr. *SRDS—The National Authority Serving the Media Buying Function*. Evanston, Ill.: Northwestern University Press, 1968. 335 pp.

Palmer, W. R. *Freelance Business Writing Business*. Monmouth Junction, N.J.: Heathcote Publishers, 1979. 303 pp.

Schiller, R. D., ed. *Market and Media Evaluation ("MAME")*. New York: Macmillan Publishing Co., 1969. 434 pp.

Shulman, J. J. *How to Get Published in Business-Professional Journals*. New York: American Management Association, Inc., 1980. 256 pp.

Simons, H., ed. *The Media and Business*. New York: Random House, Inc. (Vintage Trade Books), 1979.

Smith, C. G. *Editor's Manual—Functions and Techniques of Editing Business and Other Specialized Publications*. Second edition. Plandome, N.Y.: Cortland Gray Smith, 1969. 92 pp.

Society of Technical Writers & Publishers, Inc., and Carnegie Library of Pittsburgh. *An Annotated Bibliography on Technical Writing, Editing, Graphics, and Publishing, 1950-1965.* Pittsburgh: Society of Technical Writers & Publishers, Inc., and Carnegie Library of Pittsburgh, 1966. 322 pp.

Standard Rate & Data Service, Inc. *Business Publication Rates and Data.* Skokie, Ill.: Standard Rate & Data Service, Inc. (Published monthly.)

Turner, R. P. 1964. *Technical Writer's & Editor's Stylebook.* Indianapolis, Ind.: Howard W. Sames & Co., 1964. 208 pp.

Wall Street Journal. *The Best of the Wall Street Journal.* Homewood, Ill.: Dow-Jones-Irwin, 1974. 300 pp.

Weisman, H. M. *Basic Technical Writing.* Columbus, Ohio: Charles E. Merrill Publishing Co., 1962. 501 pp.

Wilbur, L. P. *How to Write Articles That Sell* (Self-Teaching Guides). New York: John Wiley & Sons, 1981. 217 pp.

ABP PUBLICATIONS

Available from The American Business Press, Inc. (205 E. 42 St., New York, NY 10017):

Accounting Guide
ABP Computer Guide
An Evaluation of 1100 Research Studies on the Effectiveness of Industrial Advertising, report by Arthur D. Little, Inc.
Guidelines to Editorial Budgeting, by Edgar Grunwald
Guidelines to Editorial Color, by Edgar A. Grunwald
Guidelines to Editorial Interviewing, Hiring and Firing, by Taylor J. Ogden and Betty Cannes, edited by Leslie Brennan
Guidelines to Editorial Performance, by ABP Editorial Committee
Guidelines to Editorial Research, by David P. Forsyth
A Handbook on Writing for the Dealer and Distributor
Libel: An ABP Practical Guide
Privacy and the Right of Publicity: An ABP Practical Guide

ARTICLES

Bennett, J. R., "Newspaper Reporting of U.S. Business Crime in 1980," *Newspaper Research Journal* 3:1 (October 1981) 45-53.

Bonafede, D., "The Bull Market in Business/Economics Reporting," *Washington Journalism Review* (July/August 1980).

Dominick, J. R., "Business Coverage in Network Newscasts," *Journalism Quarterly* 58:2 (Summer 1981) 179-185.

Grunig, J. E., "Developing Economic Education Programs for the Press," *Public Relations Review* 8:3 (Fall 1982) 43-62.

Hall, B., "The Brown Lung Controversy: How the Press, North and South, Handled a Story Involving the South's Largest Industry," *Columbia Journalism Review* (March/April 1978).

Rippey, J. N., "Perceptions by Selected Executives of Local Business Coverage," *Journalism Quarterly* 58:3 (Fall 1981) 382-387.

Welles, C., "Business Journalism's Glittering Prizes," *Columbia Journalism Review* (March/April 1979).

Index

227